G000229451

Pedal Portugal

CYCLING THE ALGARVE

by

Huw Thomas

Pedal Portugal Cycle Tours & Day Rides: Volume 2

First edition – 2015

Engine House Press

Cycling The Algarve

By Huw Thomas

First edition: published July 2015 by Engine House Press.

Copyright © Huw Thomas

pedalportugal.com

At a glance

What's involved

This book contains four sections.

1. **Touring Circuit:** A six-day, 329km route through the western half of the region involving:

   - overnight stops in some of the region's oldest towns and prettiest villages.
   - riding through quiet countryside and rugged, forested hills
   - visits to some of Portugal's most beautiful beaches and dramatic coastal scenery

   The route also extends into the Alentejo to include more of the South-West Alentejo and Costa Vicentina Natural Park, the biggest protected area on the country's coast.

2. **Loulé Connection:** Inland and coastal routes between Loulé and Silves: giving an option to extend the main circuit further east or to be used as two one-day rides (of 61 and 72km).

3. **Almodôvar Loop:** Two routes connecting Loulé with Almodôvar: useful for touring cyclists wanting to connect with Pedal Portugal's *Alentejo Circuit* (see page 203), or as additional day rides (of 67 and 61km).

4. **Day Rides:** A collection of 10 one-off rides starting from various towns around the western Algarve, varying in length and difficulty.

   A number use railway stations on the Faro-Lagos line as their start/finish point, giving easier access to a choice of rides.

Distances and duration

The 329km **Touring Circuit** is designed to be ridden over six days. On the other hand, riders happy to do more than 100km per day (and who don't do any of the suggested side trips) could probably complete it in as little as three days.

Adding in the **Day Rides** that start from towns on the circuit would extend the route to up to 610km.

The **Loulé Connection** and **Almodôvar Loop** give another four days of riding, totalling a further 262km.

Taking the longest options given, the 10 individual **Day Rides** add up to another 352km.

Together, this means you've got detailed directions for a total of 943km of cycling in this guidebook.

Best time to go

The Algarve provides some of the best opportunities for winter cycling anywhere in Europe. December and January can often provide days of clear blue skies and pleasant daytime riding temperatures (14-20°C).

To avoid the worst heat and crowds, the region is best between late October and early May.

Avoid June to September when afternoon temperatures can often peak at well over 40°C (104°F) and roads will be at their busiest with tourist traffic.

Typical riding

The Algarve's terrain varies from quite gentle to very rugged – and the riding on the routes described in this book is equally diverse.

The main circuit includes flatter coastal plateaus and gentle river valleys but also some major hills. The route goes from sea level to around 450m (about 1,500ft) in altitude – although an optional side trip takes in the Algarve's highest peak, Fóia, which is 902m (almost 3,000ft) above sea level.

Roads used are mostly minor and/or quiet but – where no other obvious option is available – it is necessary to ride along a few busier stretches.

Some stages involve plenty of chances to stop in towns and villages and find cafés/shops. However, a couple of days involve riding through rural areas where there are limited opportunities for buying supplies/refreshments.

Highlights

The scenery and the climate are the two most obvious attractions but the Algarve also has a rich history, involving Roman, Visigothic and Moorish influences.

Lagos was home to Europe's first slave market and the area was the base for the 15th century maritime expeditions that established Portugal as one of the western world's major sea powers.

Fish and seafood are a big feature on restaurant menus, while desserts may include locally-grown figs, carob, almonds and oranges. The Algarve is also well known for its pottery and ceramics.

With its salt pans, sea cliffs, hills and woods, the Algarve attracts a wide variety of both resident and migratory birds. Its countryside is home to many rare species – of flowers, fungi, reptiles, butterflies and other insects, and birds.

The other highlight is the people. To outsiders the Portuguese can sometimes seem a bit dour but try speaking a few words in their language (however badly) and you'll soon get a smile.

From my own experience, most Portuguese people are very friendly and happy to help visitors. They've also generally got a good sense of humour and a healthy disregard for rules.

Disclaimer

The directions – and distances – given in this book are as accurate and up to date as I can make them.

However, be aware your own measurement may vary depending on the device you're using, any detours taken – and how straight a line you ride.

I also take no responsibility for changes made to roads, junctions, signposting etc.!

Contents

MAPS INDEX

About the Algarve

Stretching across the far south of Portugal, the former Kingdom of the Algarve covers around 5,000km² (nearly 2,000m²), giving it a similar land area to the English counties of Hampshire and Berkshire combined, or the US state of Delaware.

The Algarve is bordered by the Atlantic to the west and south, Spain to the east, and Portugal's Alentejo region to the north.

People

The area's permanent population is around 450,000, making it roughly four-times as densely populated as the Alentejo.

But that permanent population is dwarfed by its visitors. The Algarve draws many more tourists than the rest of the country combined and is one of Europe's top tourism destination.

Around 3,000,000 Portuguese people and 7,000,000 foreigners visit the Algarve each year. Most visitors, though, don't stray far outside the main resort areas and barely touch what the region has to offer.

The Algarve is also the one area of Portugal where you're likely to hear non-Portuguese voices year-round. Large numbers of ex-pats (mainly British, Dutch and German) have settled here.

Some live around the resorts but many have bought properties inland, including a lot of old rural buildings.

Economy

The Algarve is the second richest area of mainland Portugal (after Lisbon), although per capita income is still only 86% of the EU average.

Apart from tourism, the biggest industries today are building/development (mostly tourism-related), horticulture and fisheries.

Traditional agriculture – growing oranges, figs, carobs, olives, grapes and almonds – has declined. Although the fertile coastal strip remains fairly prosperous, inland many rural properties lie abandoned; fields and hillsides once cultivated have been taken over by cistus bushes and other scrub.

History

Historically, human presence in the Algarve dates back to the Stone Age. Early tribes established themselves inland around the 6th century BC, while the Carthaginian and Phoenicians set up trading posts along the coast, including at modern-day Portimão.

The Romans arrived in the 2nd century BC: the ruins of a large villa at Milreu to the north of Faro form one of the region's premier archaeological sites.

The Visigoths came next, followed by the Muslim conquest early in the 8th century; the name 'Algarve' derives from the Arabic *Al-Gharb*, which simply means 'the west'.

The Moors occupied the Algarve for around five centuries, building castles and establishing many towns. Then came the Christian 're-conquest' as Crusaders led by the King of Portugal drove out the Moors.

The Algarve kept its unique identity for centuries; up until the declaration of the Portuguese Republic in 1910, the country's official name was 'the United Kingdom of Portugal, Brazil and the Algarves'.

Maritime expeditions launched from the Lagos area in the 15th century not only led to major discoveries by Portuguese navigators but also helped establish Portugal as one of the world's sea powers. Lagos became the first centre of the European slave trade.

In 1755 the earthquake that flattened Lisbon also left many Algarve towns, including Lagos, severely damaged by the huge tremors and subsequent tsunami.

Protected by lagoons, Faro was not as devastated and subsequently took over as the regional capital. During the Peninsula War, Spanish troops occupied the Algarve but were driven out again within a couple of years.

Faro, which lies only just over half a degree north of Tunis in North Africa, today has a population of around 44,000 in its actual urban area. Portimão is slightly bigger with around 45,000 inhabitants.

Cycling in the Algarve

The Algarve has some excellent cycling – if you know when and where to go.

There are plenty of over-developed resorts all along the coast. In the summer these can be extremely busy but it's also then generally way too hot for any serious cycling.

But the resorts only make up a tiny proportion of the Algarve. There are many roads further inland that see few visitors at any time of the year.

As well as offering some of the best winter cycling opportunities anywhere in Europe, the Algarve has some wonderful scenery, from wild hill country to dramatic, untouched beaches.

There are valleys to follow, countryside to explore, and villages to visit. Then there are all the other attractions: the sunshine, the food, the history, the flora and fauna, the wine...

Below I've attempted to detail some of the issues, both positive and negative, relevant to cycling in the region.

Terrain

The Algarve's landscape is extremely varied. Stick to the coastal strip and you'll encounter no major hills; turn north and things very quickly get much more rugged.

Dividing the Algarve and the Alentejo, the highest mountains are north of Lagos, where the Serra de Monchique rises to 902m.

Inland from Faro, the Serra do Caldeirão and the Serra do Malhão reach a maximum of 577m.

Further east the hills aren't as high but the terrain is possibly even more rugged. A couple of fairly deep valleys, separated by high ridges, run west-east to join the Rio Guadiana, which forms the border with Spain.

Running along the coast from close to the Spanish border to just west of Faro is a series of sand bars, islands and lagoons that separate the land and sea, forming the Parque Natural da Ria Formosa.

From Albufeira west, the coast turns into a series of rocky headlands separating some truly gorgeous beaches, which are one of the big draws for all those millions of tourists.

Beyond Lagos the coast gets progressively wilder as it approaches Cabo de São Vicente, the south-west point of the European mainland.

North of the cape, the Algarve's west coast is even more dramatic but much harder to access – meaning it also attracts a fraction of the number of visitors.

Between the coast and the mountains, much of the Algarve's interior is characterised by hills covered with a mixture of forestry (eucalyptus and pine plantations) and cistus scrub.

Expanses of cork oak and orchards of citrus trees, almonds, carobs, figs and olives also cover some areas of both hills and valleys. However, these crops are in decline and some orchards have been left to go wild.

The relatively small areas where most of the region's farming and horticulture takes place are generally undulating, with reasonable hills in some places, rather than flat.

The easiest cycling in the Algarve (although still not entirely flat) is probably to be found around some of the beach resorts between Quarteira and Portimão, or between Faro and Tavira to the east. However, these are generally the busiest and most built-up parts of the region.

Alternatively, the inland area between Silves, São Bartolomeu de Messines and Loulé, probably offers the best compromise in terms of relatively gentle terrain and quieter roads.

When to go

Unless you're used to the heat, cycling in the Algarve between May and September is not the best choice in Portugal. Go north!

Late autumn can offer good cycling conditions; October is generally still pretty hot, with temperatures cooling in November. The only downside is that the countryside can look very harsh and barren at this time of year.

Winter (December to January) can offer perfect conditions, with clear skies and temperatures ranging around 15-25°C (60-80°F), making it feel more like a summer's day in northern Europe.

On 'bad' days, the Algarve in winter feels more like England in spring, with a mix of heavy showers, sunny spells and stiff breezes. You can get days of rain but it rarely sets in for long.

Prevailing winds are from the north. Strong, cold winds can be a feature of some January days, but get out of them and you'll generally be basking in the sunshine.

Early spring (February to April) is when the landscape is at its greenest and the flowers at their best. Showers are a danger; longer spells of rain are not impossible but less likely. Temperatures will build steadily through March and it can already be getting seriously hot again as you move into April.

Roads & traffic

The coastal areas of the Algarve are generally served by a good network of roads, ranging from busy main roads to small lanes.

However, as you go further north and inland, your choices get more limited and there are large areas of hill country with very few roads of any kind.

Other than motorways, the main transport route across the region is the N125, which runs all the way from Spain to Vila do Bispo in the west.

Traffic, including lots of HGVs and other commercial vehicles, is generally heaviest around Faro but anywhere on the coast between Lagos and Tavira is liable to be busy. The areas around

Faro, Portimão and (to a lesser extent) Loulé are the most densely populated parts of the Algarve.

Routes to some inland tourist destinations – e.g. the N266 to Monchique – may also get busy with cars and coaches at weekends and during the holiday season.

The only other main transport route likely to have a fair level of commercial traffic is the IC1, which parallels the motorway from north of Albufeira towards Lisbon.

While many rural roads are quiet for much of the year, you may occasionally experience heavy traffic if forestry operations are being carried out in the area or crops are being harvested.

For cyclists wanting to explore the region the biggest difficulties are avoiding the busier roads nearer the coast and finding sealed back roads. The limited road network can also make planning circular routes more tricky inland.

It's also important to realise that road designations often give little indication of how busy a road actually is. You might expect the N2 to be a major national highway. In fact, once you get away from the section joining Faro with the A22 motorway, it's little more than a twisting (and scenic) back road.

Portuguese roads can have a confusing number of designations. The main ones are summarised below:

A: motorways – off-limits to cyclists
N: 'national' roads – includes major **and** minor roads
E: European routes – includes A and N roads
IP: 'principal' roads – includes both A and N roads – sometimes but not always closed to cyclists
IC: 'complementary' – includes both A and N roads – sometimes but not always closed to cyclists

Other designations you may see include EN (short for *estrada nacional* and another term for N roads), R (regional) and M, EM or CM (municipal roads).

With N roads, those starting with 1 were originally the most important. Those beginning with 2 were secondary and those with a hyphen (e.g. N125-4) were branch roads. However, this 1945 system is largely redundant as many roads originally given a 1 are now minor routes of little importance.

Road surfaces

Road surfaces within the Algarve vary from excellent to rough but are generally better than in many areas of the UK.

A lot of European money has been spent on Portuguese roads and many principal routes, plus some secondary ones, have had extensive upgrades over the past couple of decades.

Even on major routes traffic levels are low compared to much of northern Europe, giving the added advantage that surfaces don't tend to wear out as quickly.

However, some roads in coastal areas get relatively high levels of commercial and tourist traffic and can be worn in places. In rural areas roads may be rough because they have never been sealed properly or because of damage from agricultural vehicles.

On the plus side, some roads still marked as unsealed on old maps have been surfaced in recent years.

One problem in the Algarve is landslips and subsidence can turn road surfaces into a roller coaster of dips and humps – sometimes with a road edge that has disappeared down the hillside.

Newer roads tend to have very smooth tarmac that is a pleasure to ride upon, while older back roads, particularly in rural areas, get patched much more crudely.

Each municipal authority has responsibility for its own local roads so you may also find a road suddenly go from extremely rough to very smooth (or vice versa) as you cross the border between municipalities.

The worst problem for cyclists is in town centres and villages. The Portuguese love cobbles: big hard-wearing chunks of rough granite that can look pretty from a distance.

The granite cobbles are a real pain – literally – to ride on. I did a one-year tour around France, Spain and Portugal, and had several problems with bits on my bike literally shaking apart in Portugal. (And that's not to mention the wear to my backside and wrists.)

Pavements (sidewalks) aren't much better as they are often paved in limestone blocks that are equally uneven and can be lethally slick when wet.

Outside the towns, the vast majority of roads mentioned in this guide are sealed.

Maps

I've been on a quest to discover the best printed maps of Portugal for a long time and have come to the conclusion that accurate, detailed, up-to-date ones simply don't exist.

It can also be difficult to find even halfway decent printed maps in Portugal. Most shops only have tourist maps that show very limited detail.

If you want a map just for an overview, then Michelin's 1:400,000 map of Portugal is reasonable, although it leaves off some back roads and many geographical features (like reservoirs) are decades out of date.

(There is a 1:300,000 Michelin edition covering the south of the country but as far as I can tell it is just a blown-up version of part of the national map and provides no additional information.)

The most accurate topographical maps are military maps produced by the Instituto Geografico do Exercito (see www.igeoe.pt). However, the scale (1:25,000 or 1:50,000) makes them too detailed for cycling further than short distances.

The design and way the contours are printed also makes the IGE maps hard to read and they're years out of date. Lots of old back roads are shown but most roads built in the past few decades are missing.

A Portuguese company called Forways produces a 1:215,000 Algarve map that you can pick up locally for €5.50. However, while this shows a bit more detail than Michelin it's not completely trustworthy. Some roads (and villages) are in the wrong place, some are shown as sealed when they're not.

The Forway's map is okay to get a general idea of where places are but don't rely on it for navigating.

If you want a printed map while cycling, I'd either take the Michelin map for a limited overview or buy a road atlas and remove the relevant pages. (This is generally not much more expensive and is about as lightweight as you can get.)

However, if you want to do any navigating on routes not covered in this guide then online options – e.g. OpenStreetMap (OSM) or Google – are far more detailed, accurate and up to date than anything you can buy on paper.

If you're happy to stick with the rides in this guide, then the directions it contains – plus the maps provided – should give enough details for you to find your way around quite comfortably.

For more information on the maps contained in this guide (and online versions), see **What's in the Guide** below (page 21).

Signposts & navigating

To be blunt, signposting in Portugal is extremely poor; and where it exists, often erratic and hard to follow.

This isn't so much of a problem in the countryside if you're on N roads as there is generally – although not always – a sign at most major junctions. Minor roads may be more problematic and junctions sometimes completely unmarked.

Some major roads (though not many in the Algarve) have kilometre markers that show you the road number and the distance to towns in either direction.

Be aware, though, that the road's designation letter may be out of date if it has been up or downgraded. The number, however, should have stayed the same.

Towns are generally the biggest headache. You may get a signpost as you arrive in town and then nothing at the next junction.

Some streets have their names on signs but many don't, so finding your way can involve a fair bit of luck even when you know what you're looking for.

However, there are two rules that work *most* of the time. One is: if you're trying to follow a signposted direction and all signs disappear, just keep following whatever looks like the most major route. You'll generally pick up the route again a bit further on.

The second rule is, if trying to find the middle of town, aim for the church. As well as being in the centre, there's a fair chance the roads leading from it will be signposted.

And don't worry if you can't speak the lingo: most Portuguese people will go out of their way to help a visitor, particularly if you can at least say 'please' (*por favour*) in their language.

Heat & light

The heat can be extreme if you're in the Algarve between early May and the end of September.

Don't be misled by daily *average* figures: afternoon temperatures of well over 40°C (100°F) are typical in the summer and it can often be above 30°C (90°F) in spring and autumn. (See **When to go** on page 13 for more details).

Light levels are another important factor for cyclists. This is one of the southernmost regions of Europe – almost on a par with North Africa – and the sun can get intense.

I would strongly recommend a good pair of wrap-around sunglasses – and a peak/visor on your cycle helmet to give your eyes some shade.

Accommodation

Accommodation in Portugal is generally cheap and extremely good value compared to most other European countries. The Algarve is more expensive than the rest of Portugal but still relatively cheap.

A lot of the easiest accommodation to find when touring is in guest houses (*pensões* and *residenciais*), which generally offer the best deals.

Hotels, particularly 2* and 3*, are often not much more expensive. Prices will also vary depending how busy a town is and how many establishments are competing for your trade.

If you want an authentic 'Portuguese' feel, *turismo rural* properties can offer a stay at somewhere a bit more special, often in more out of the way locations, albeit generally at a higher price.

Hotels and guest houses

Although there is a huge amount of holiday accommodation in the Algarve, most is aimed at people coming for one or two-week holidays. High visitor numbers will also mean rooms are at a premium in peak season.

Although some places shut over the winter, many stay open and most hotels and guest houses will be quiet between November and March, meaning you should not only have more choice but hopefully be able to find some bargains.

Out of season, you should be able to get a single room in a basic guest house for €25 (or less). For a few more frills, €30-40 should be enough. Above €50 euros and you can expect quite a high standard. (Add 20% or so for summer prices/a double room.)

Local council/tourist websites can provide useful lists of accommodation – links are given in the appropriate sections.

If you want to book in advance I'd recommend a site like booking.com

If you just turn up on the day, most towns have a tourist office that can help (although opening hours can vary). However, you may find the best deals yourself by looking for rooms advertised in private houses or above restaurants, look for signs advertising *quartos* or *dormidas*.

Another great source of online bargains is airbnb.co.uk – where you can search for accommodation on a very slick and easy-to-use website that puts you in direct touch with owners.

Accommodation on AirBnB ranges from rooms in private homes to self-catering flats or holiday villas, and you can read reviews from other travellers.

Camping:

Many campsites, particularly those on the coast, are also set up to deal with hordes of visitors in the summer months. Space will be at an absolute premium in July and August and you may need to book in advance – some sites also insist on a minimum stay of several days (or a week) in peak season.

Some campsites are also mainly set up for caravans and motorhomes, some of which are parked on site all year round. On these sites, even though they look enormous, you may find the area provided for tent camping is very small.

Larger campsites can also be busy in spring and summer catering for the large numbers of ex-pats who come to the Algarve for the sunshine and low cost of living.

Space is less likely to be at a premium at smaller campsites and those inland, particularly outside July and August.

Most Algarve campsites are open year-round but do check if going there out of the main holiday season.

Hospitality networks:

Some cyclists have already discovered the hospitality available through www.warmshowers.org

Hosts on the worldwide network generally offer a free bed for the night (and a shower) to travelling cyclists.

Apart from being a host myself (previously in Portugal and now in the UK) I've been a guest in half a dozen countries and have met some wonderfully kind and hospitable people.

There's a similar site called Couchsurfing that's open to all travellers but Warmshowers is purely for cyclists.

What's in the guide

The preceding section gives a general flavour of what's involved in cycling in the Algarve. The following information explains how the guide is laid out.

Touring Circuit, Loulé Connection & Almodôvar Loop

These sections each begin with information on that ride's start point, including:

- an **overview** of the town involved
- notes on **transport links** and ways of getting to the start point
- examples of **accommodation**

The main notes are then broken down into individual riding 'days', each one containing:

1. **Overview**: This gives a short description of what's involved in that day's ride, highlighting any alternative routes or side trips and giving an overview map.

2. **Stats**: Key figures for the day's ride, including distance, total elevation gain, maximum incline (gradient) and ride profile.

   This section also includes a links to an online map that can be downloaded in different formats (e.g. GPX files) from www.ridewithgps.com

3. **Directions**: Each day is divided into logical, numbered stages, with the total distance (in km) at the start of each section.

   The numbered stages highlight every junction where you need to change direction, and any other significant features.

4. **Notes**: Background information on places to visit/sites of interest is included in the directions at the relevant place.

   Where there are long sections without many villages or towns, I have tried to identify cafés, restaurants and shops that may provide useful stops.

5. **Supermarkets & bike shops**: These are identified within the directions, as well as in the notes on each overnight stop.

6. **Alternative routes**: Suggestions for possible alternative cycling options are outlined in the overview, with details (if necessary) following the directions for the main route.

7. **Side trips**: Ideas for places to visit/detours along the way are included at appropriate places in the main directions.

   Additional rides from the end/start points of individual stages are included in the **Day Rides** section.

8. **Maps**: More detailed maps of towns/villages along the route of the **Touring Circuit** are included immediately following the directions for each day.

   Maps for the **Loulé Connection** and **Almodôvar Loop** are included at the end of each of these sections.

   All these maps are taken from www.openstreetmap.org

   Arrows show direction of travel or indicate places of interest (e.g. supermarkets). A black circle shows the start/end of the day's ride (as given in the directions).

9. **Overnight stops**: The information for each suggested overnight stop includes:

   - General facts and description of the town
   - Where to find supermarkets, bike shops or other useful facilities
   - Accommodation options, including campsites and examples of guest houses/hotels
   - Links to town hall or tourist office websites containing local accommodation listings

   Note: Information on accommodation is there for reference only – these are NOT recommendations unless clearly indicated otherwise.

   Those places that myself or other riders *can* recommend are marked with a * before their name, e.g. ***Hotel Marina Rio**.

Day Rides

This section is slightly different as it assumes you've already got a base and concentrates on the ride itself, each of which is listed under the name of the town where they start and finish.

For a number of day rides, I've used railway stations as the start/finish point.

That's because the regional line from Lagos to Faro (and further east) is a great way of getting to different places from which to ride. Tickets are cheap, bicycles go free and there's a large guards' van with space for plenty of bikes.

Be aware, however, that train stations are often several kilometres from the town they are named after.

Most rides are circuits, although a couple are 'there and back'.

A short introduction describing the ride and terrain etc. is followed by a **stats** section as above.

Detailed **directions** then guide you around the ride, broken down into numbered stages with individual distances.

Immediately following the directions you will find details of **maps** that may be of use, including for start/finish points and towns/villages on route.

Some of the maps referred to are those used earlier in the book – additional maps for locations not previously covered are contained at the end of the Day Rides section. (There is also an alphabetical Maps Index on page eight.)

Please note: arrows shown on maps from the Touring Circuit relate to that route and not to the Day Rides.

TOURING CIRCUIT

Overview

This circuit takes in the full range of the Algarve's scenery – from a climb into its highest mountain range, to the wild beaches of the west coast, the resort town of Lagos and the orange groves and pastures of the rural interior.

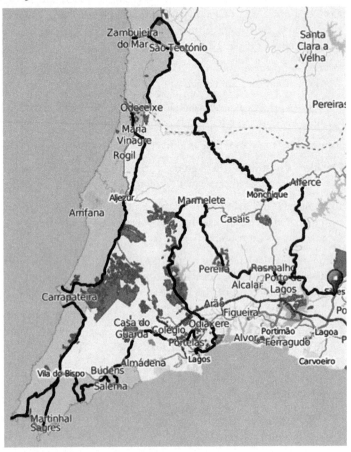

Map adapted from OpenStreetMap, created via ridewithgps.com
For details, see: www.ridewithgps.com/routes/7358240

Designed as a six-day tour (see **Stages** below), the circuit starts and finishes in Silves, once the Moorish capital of the Al-Gharb kingdom, now a quiet riverside town.

There's also plenty of flexibility: add in some extra day rides and you've got around a dozen days of cycling, including exploring further north up the Alentejo coast.

Alternatively, those who want to ride harder and further each day can skip the extras, leave out some stops and get round in three to four days.

It isn't all easy riding; the first day's climb to Monchique involves ascending from sea level to around 450m (1,500ft). However, none of the days are impossibly long and there are few inclines of any length steeper than 10%.

The scenery is also some of the best you'll find anywhere in Portugal's far south west.

As well as hills, you'll see pretty villages, historic towns, dramatic cliffs, stunning beaches and plenty of quiet countryside.

Distance & difficulty

The total distance is 329km (206 miles), or 610km (381 miles) if you add in all the possible side trips from the towns on the circuit.

The first day to Monchique involves an unavoidable big climb. However, there are two options for tackling it: a tough but incredibly scenic way and an alternative route that's busier but a lot more gentle.

The only other day involving a major climb is the last one, going from Lagos back to Silves. In this case, however, there is an alternative route that completely avoids any mountains and is relatively gentle (and almost half the distance).

All the other days involve some hills but nothing of any size or involving extreme gradients. (The profile on the previous page may look scary but that's only because it's compressed to fit the total distance on one line.)

Road surfaces are mixed: generally good but you will have to watch out for dips and bumps on some sections and rough surfaces on others. This, however, is generally the price you pay for the best scenery or avoiding a section of busy road.

Most of the roads used on this circuit are minor with few commercial vehicles, although you may have to watch out for tourist traffic at busy times.

There are a few busier sections but only where unavoidable and still safe. The area around Lagos is likely to be the busiest section on this circuit.

Heat is the other biggest problem that could affect cyclists in the Algarve. Please make sure you read about **When to go** in the introduction (page 13).

Stages

The main route has been broken down into six days.

1. Silves to Monchique 37km (23 miles)
2. Monchique to Zambujeira 53.5km (33.5 miles)
3. Zambujeira to Aljezur 49.5km (31 miles)
4. Aljezur to Sagres 60.3km (38 miles)
5. Sagres to Lagos 54.7km (34 miles)
6. Lagos to Silves 73.5km (46 miles)

Although most of these days are fairly short for anyone used to riding long distances, there are opportunities to extend each day – except the fifth one – using the **Day Rides** described in the last section of the book.

Days Two to Five also provide many opportunity for visiting some wonderful stretches of coast, so you may want to mix some beach time in with your cycling.

Quicker version

If you want to cut the number of days, the simplest thing to knock off a day would be to ride from Silves to Zambujeira in one go.

This would definitely be a challenge. Not only is it the first day but it involves the biggest climb. From Monchique, though, there's a lot of downhill to get to the coast and only one other hill of any size. Total ascent over the day would probably be around 600m.

Cutting out a couple of beach detours between Zambujeira and Aljezur and taking a straighter route would reduce this stage from 49.5km to 35.1km.

You could also skip Zambujeira, stay in the Algarve, and go straight from Monchique to Aljezur.

Extended version

Alternatively, if you've got time to spend more than one day in each place you could easily extend the tour to 12 days (and 610km) as follows:

1. Silves to Monchique – 37km (23 miles)
2. Fóia day ride – 17.5km (11 miles)
3. Monchique to Zambujeira – 53.5km (33.5 miles)
4. Cabo Sardão day ride – 42km – (26.5 miles)
5. Zambujeira to Aljezur – 49.5km (31 miles)
6. Arrifana and/or Amoreira day rides – 44km (27.5 miles)
7. Aljezur to Sagres – 60.3km (38 miles)
8. Sagres to Lagos – 54.7km (34 miles)
9. Barragem da Bravura day ride – 32.7km (20 miles)
10. Mexilhoeira day rides (train from Lagos) – 22.4km (14 miles)
11. Lagos to Silves – 73.5km (46 miles)
12. Silves Day Ride – 59.5km (37 miles)

If you want to extend your tour further, you can add in the **Loulé Connection** (see page 96) and the **Almodôvar Loop** (page 128) to give another four days of riding.

Start Point

Silves (pop. approx 11,000) is a day trip destination for most visitors to the Algarve, drawn by its picturesque riverside setting, compact old town and ruined castle.

Back in the 10th century this was one of the most important towns in the Al-Gharb, which roughly corresponds to the current Algarve and formed part of the huge area of Muslim Iberia occupied by the Moors.

The origins of Silves probably date back to Roman times and there's plenty of evidence of Palaeolithic settlement in the area.

Known as the 'Baghdad of the West' while home to the Moors, the town was first conquered by King Sanchez I of Portugal in 1189 with the help of an army of Crusaders. It was retaken by the Moors but fell again to the Christian forces in 1242, after which its Great Mosque was converted into Silves Cathedral.

The town never regained its former glory, losing out to Lagos and then Faro as the region's main town.

However, Silves retains plenty to see, including parts of its red Moorish walls. A redundant cork factory – known as the *Fabrica do Inglês* (Englishman's Factory) – is now a cultural centre, while the archaeological museum contains exhibits from the town's long history.

The castle (*Fortaleza*) looks more impressive from outside than in. More interesting for a wander is the network of streets between the riverside and the cathedral (*Sé*).

Supermarkets

There's a **Lidl** just off the N124 on the riverside going north-east out of town and a **Continenté** on the same road going west.

There's also a branch of local chain **Alisuper** on one of the streets (Rua Dr. Nobre Oliveira) on the western side of the old town.

Transport links

Train:

If you are bringing your own bike and starting the ride from Silves, the easiest way to get there is by train.

The regional service that runs from Vila Real de Santo António on the Spanish border to Lagos in the west has a large baggage compartment with special hooks for holding bikes – which travel free.

From Faro, Comboios de Portugal (www.cp.pt) runs around eight services a day to Silves. Trains take around 1hr 15mins and tickets currently cost €5.15.

From my experience, the baggage compartment is always at the west-bound (Lagos) end of the train.

Getting your bike up isn't always easy as the door is a good metre above the platform. Fortunately, the guard will normally help open the door and lift your bike up/down.

The only problem in Faro is that getting to the train station from the airport involves about 6km of very busy, motorway-standard dual carriageways.

There are wide shoulders most of the way (watch out on slip roads) but you might want to see if you can find a taxi driver to take you and your bike.

Silves train station is a couple of km outside the town. It's an easy ride, though. Simply head north (uphill), go straight on at the roundabout and follow the road down and to the right – you'll see the town on the other side of the river.

Bus:

There are local buses between Portimão and some of the other small towns in the area but no direct services between Faro, Lagos or any of the other bigger towns.

You're also unlikely to be able to take a bike on any of the local buses.

Bicycle:

If coming from the east, the **Loulé Connection** (see page 96) gives two possible routes. It is possible to ride from Faro (see notes on page 106) but roads around the Algarve's big city can be very busy and not great for cycling.

Accommodation

Camping:

The nearest campsite is 3.5km west of town off the N124 Lagos road. It's a small riverside site on terraces in an orange orchard.

Quinta da Rocha Branca, 8300-026 Silves.
Tel: 967 659 700 *Email:* info@camping-silves.com
Open: All year.

Hotels & Guest Houses:

Hotel Colina dos Mouros (3*), Estrada Nacional 269, 8300-135 Silves.
Tel: 282 440 420 *Email:* geralreservas@colinahotels.com
Web: colinahotels.com

Residencial Vila Sodré, Estrada Cruz de Portugal 124, 8300 Silves.
Tel: 282 443 441. *Email:* vilasodre@gmail.com
Web: residencialvilasodre.pt

Residencial Ladeira, Ladeira de São Pedro.
Tel: 282 442 870

For more options, including for the surrounding area, visit:
cm-silves.pt/portal_autarquico/silves/v_pt-
PT/menu_turista/Turismo/Guia+Turistico/Alojamento/

DAY ONE: SILVES – MONCHIQUE

Overview

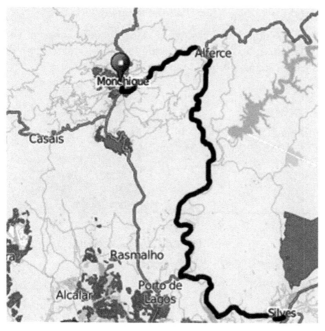

Today's ride is quite short but one of the two toughest in the circuit in terms of climbing: Silves is only just above sea level, while Monchique is at an altitude of around 440m (1,450ft).

The main route begins with 9.6km on the N124 towards Lagos. You then turn onto a fabulous back road that starts off as a fairly easy ride but is followed by nearly 7km of almost relentless climbing, reaching a maximum gradient of over 18%.

Along the way, there's a chance to stop for tours and tastings at a local vineyard – see the notes on the **Quinta do Francés** at the end of the day's directions (page 36).

If you do chose the main route, the compensation for the sweat involved is the magnificent scenery and views, which get progressively better as you head higher into the hills.

The last 8km or so into Monchique are also fairly gentle, with the road hugging the contour line for the last part.

The day's ride begins on the N124 at the bottom of town, opposite the old bridge (*Ponte Romana*) across the Rio Arade.

It ends in the attractive hill town of Monchique – although you might also want to consider a stop in the spa at Caldas de Monchique (see **First Night** on page 39 for details).

Stats

Distance: 37km
Total elevation gain: +846m/-409m
Maximum incline: 18.4%

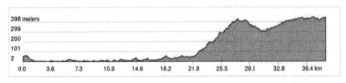

To download a map with full ride profile, available as .gpx file etc., see: ridewithgps.com/routes/7274270

Alternative routes

A shorter option – which cuts out about 250m of climbing – involves simply following the N124 and N266.

This is a much gentler route on a smoother surface but the N266 can be a lot busier and the views, although pleasant, aren't anything like as dramatic or far-reaching.

A second alternative route goes via Caldas de Monchique – see below for details.

Extension/side trip

If you've got the energy left for a 17.5km circuit (and a 450m climb), you can extend the day by continuing to the summit of the Algarve's highest mountain, Fóia.

For details see the entry listed in the **Day Rides** section under Monchique on page 182.

DIRECTIONS: SILVES – MONCHIQUE

1. **(9.6km)** Follow the N124 west (towards Lagos), going straight on at the first roundabout and past a Continenté **supermarket**.

   The surface is quite rough in parts as you leave Silves but this road doesn't generally get too much traffic.

   The scenery soon becomes more rural and, after a small hill, the road turns north-west and drops down to follow the upper section of the Rio Odelouca estuary.

   Birdwatchers will find plenty of opportunities to pull off and look for waterfowl etc. along this stretch.

   There are a few turnings off but stick on the N124 until the road turns west again and crosses the Odelouca.

2. **(10.3km)** Turn right immediately after the bridge next to a café – sadly now derelict. The road here is one-way for about 400m.

Note: If doing this route in reverse, you need to turn right at the northern end of the one-way section. The road goes up a bit of a hill before swinging south and joining the N124 a few hundred metres west of the bridge over the Odelouca.

The route now continues roughly north, following a valley scattered with small farms and orchards of orange and lemon trees. The hillsides to either side are mostly covered by a mix of pine trees, eucalyptus and cistus scrub.

There's one small hill early on to help test your legs – with a vineyard near the top (see notes on **Quinta do Francés** on page 36). A second hill near the hamlet of Monchicão is a little more testing but this is still just the warm up.

3. **(4.1km)** After the ride up the valley, you'll reach a junction with a new road going off right, with an orange sign to the *Barragem de Odelouca*.

   Keep going straight on, following the road up and around the bend to the left. This is the start of the climb.

   The ascent is steady to over the first kilometre (mostly around 7-9%). There's a brief respite (and short downhill) after going through a small cutting.

There are some excellent views off to the right here, looking down over the Odelouca reservoir and back towards the coast.

The road soon begins to climb more steeply (up to 16%) through a section of eucalyptus plantations, plus some pine and cork oak trees as the road levels off briefly while approaching a turning for the hamlet of Fornalha.

4. **(4.4km)** There's an **alternative** route from here towards Caldas de Monchique (details below).

Otherwise keep straight on past the Fornalha turning.

It's 1.6km to the top, which comes just after a viewpoint (*miradouro*) on the right.

There's one more dip and rise in the road, after which the scenery gets even prettier as you begin to drop down past terraced fields and woods towards a T-junction near the village of Alferce.

5. **(350m)** If you want a break, or just to admire the view, turn right for the village: there are several **cafés/ snack bars** in the centre. Otherwise, go left and follow the road down to another T-junction on the N267.

6. **(7.4km)** Turn left on the N267, which is signposted 'Monchique' and 'Portimão'. The road dips and then climbs for a while but it's a good road surface and only a very gentle incline.

If the weather's good, you should have marvellous views across the small villages in the valley below and the hills of the Serra de Monchique.

The road climbs to about 440m above sea level before following the contour line towards Monchique.

You come down to a roundabout on the N266, opposite an Intermarché **supermarket**.

7. **(800m)** Turn right onto the N266/Rua Serpa Pinto. The road splits a short way along, bear right to follow the one-way system up into town.

The road splits at a T-junction, which marks the end of the day's ride. For the next day's stage go right. For the centre of town and the way to Fóia follow the road left and up the hill.

Alternative routes

1.

For a much easier (and shorter) climb up to Monchique the route is quite simple.

Follow the N124 west-bound towards Lagos. After 11.8km you'll come to a roundabout at a junction with the N266. Turn right here and it's about 16.5km to the edge of Monchique.

The N266 gets quite a lot more traffic. It isn't nose-to-tail cars but Monchique attracts quite a few day trippers from the coast, particularly for the the markets held on the second Monday of each month and at weekends.

It is also only two-lane and fairly narrow in places. On the plus side, the road is well-surfaced and there is a shoulder wide enough to ride on in some sections.

Another advantage of this route is that it also takes you past the thermal spa at Caldas de Monchique.

2.

If you have ridden up towards Alferce but want to go via Caldas, there's another **alternative** route.

If you turn left at the **Fornalha** junction, a small but extremely scenic road wiggles around the south side of the hill. The surface is quite rough and broken up in places but it is rideable.

There are also a few ups and downs – none very long but some quite steep going this way. However, the views back towards the coast are stunning on a clear day.

The road will eventually bring you out on the N266 immediately above Caldas.

Quinta do Francés

If you want to investigate vine growing and winemaking in the Algarve, then the Quinta do Francés might be worth a visit.

The vineyard is just off your route on the first day – although bearing in mind the size of the hill to follow, you might want to visit on a separate occasion, possibly as a minor detour while on the way back to Silves from Lagos.

In production since 2008, the quinta has eight hectares of vines and offers tours and tastings at the winery. Franco-Italian winemaker Patrick Agostini has won medals for two of his wines.

The entrance to Quinta do Francés is about 1km along the Alferce road from the turning off the N124 by the Odelouca bridge.

See www.quintadofrances.com for more information.

MAPS: DAY ONE

1. Silves – start point

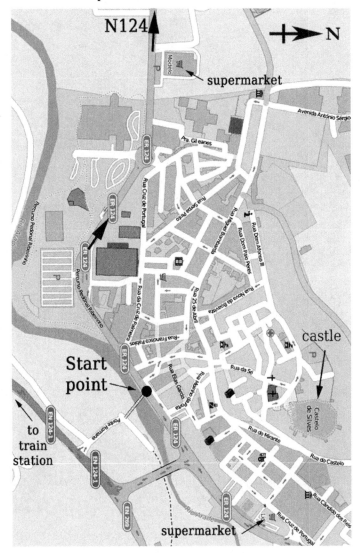

2. Monchique

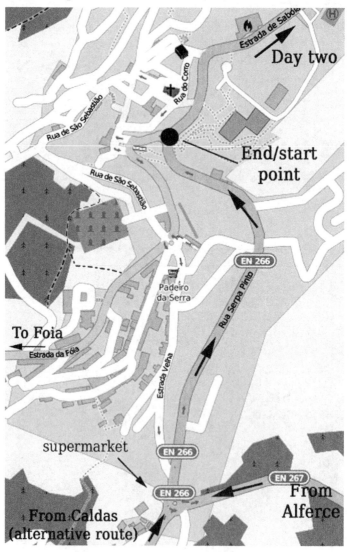

FIRST NIGHT

Monchique (pop 4,800) is a small town, most famous for its market, held on the second Monday of each month. (This is in addition to a smaller market that takes place every Sunday.)

The town is also known for the production of *Medronho*, an Algarvean liqueur made from the fruit of the strawberry tree (arbutus). If you're there in March, carnivores may also be interested in the town's traditional Sausage Fair.

In addition to the attractions mentioned above, Monchique's elevation means it provides a good opportunity to escape the heat down on the coast and it can get busy at weekends and in the main holiday season.

Out of season, it's still quite sleepy and remains a pleasant place for a wander. There are no major sights but the town has some attractive old buildings and plenty of small cobbled streets to explore as they wind around the hillside.

You can also walk to a ruined 17th century convent above the town. The path going up to the right just before the building is part of a long distance walking route to the summit of Fóia.

Supermarkets

The **Intermarché** off the roundabout on the N266 to the south of town is the only supermarket of any size. There are several *mini-mercados* and other shops in the centre itself.

Accommodation

Camping:

There is no campsite in the immediate area.

Hotels & Guest houses:

Hospedaria Decansa Pernas, 8550-427 Monchique. *Tel:* 282 913 170

Inn Bica Boa, Estrada Nacional 266, 8550 Monchique. *Tel:* 282 912 271 *Email:* bica-boa@sapo.pt *Web:* bicaboa.com

Miradouro da Serra, Rua dos Combatentes do Ultramar, 8550-459 Monchique. *Tel:* 282 912 163

For more options, including hotels and other properties in the surrounding area, see:
cm-monchique.pt/portal_autarquico/monchique/v_pt-PT/menu_turista/turismo/Onde+Dormir/

Caldas de Monchique has been known since Roman times for its spa waters. Set in a narrow valley, four springs provide mineral-rich water at up to 32°C (90°F).

Once popular with Portuguese royalty, the spa's 19th century buildings had gone into a bit of a decline but underwent a major restoration in 2000.

The spa and hotel are closed in January and half of February – unfortunate as a soak in its hot water might be particularly appreciated in the winter. (**Note**: please also check opening times at the end of the year.)

While the spa is open, it would probably make a worthwhile visit. Its hotel could also make a pleasant alternative to Monchique itself for an overnight stay if you want to splash out a bit. Non-hotel guests can also use the spa facilities (for a fee) and there's also a nearby inn offering accommodation.

Accommodation

Hotels & Guest Houses:

Vila Termal das Caldas de Monchique, Caldas de Monchique, 8550-232 Monchique.
Tel: 282 910 910 *Email:* reservas@monchiquetermas.com
Web: monchiquetermas.com

Albergaria do Lageado, Caldas de Monchique, 8550-232 Monchique.
Tel: 282 912 616 *Email:* info@albergariadolageado.com
Web: albergariadolageado.com

For more options – including rooms (*quartos*) in private homes – see the turismo link at the bottom of the Monchique listings.

DAY TWO: MONCHIQUE – ZAMBUJEIRA

Overview

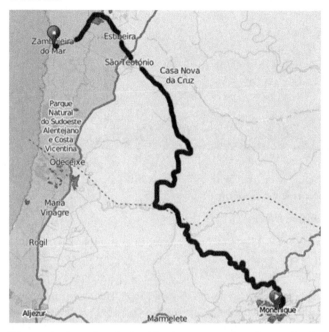

The majority of today's ride is very rural and mostly, but not entirely, downhill.

Leaving Monchique, you soon turn on to a minor road that takes you west along a twisting route through eucalyptus forest.

The road is mostly fairly level to begin with then turns north-west and drops down bend after bend towards the Ribeira de Seixe, which forms the frontier between the Algarve and the Alentejo.

After following the Seixe for a way, the route crosses the river – entering the Alentejo region – and heads north. This is where you have the one big climb of the day and the steepest section of ascent.

Once up the other side of the valley, you follow an undulating route through a mixture of farmland and forested hills towards the small town of São Teotónio, after which the riding gets a lot flatter for the last section out towards the coast and the pretty village of Zambujeira do Mar.

Stats

Distance: 53.5km
Total elevation gain: +624m/-1,024m
Maximum incline: 15%

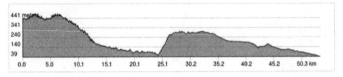

To download a map with full ride profile, available as .gpx file etc., see: ridewithgps.com/routes/7283767

Alternative routes

If you're short of time and don't want to go up into the Alentejo, one option is to go straight from Monchique to Aljezur and pick up the route from **Day Three**.

Anyone who doesn't mind a bit of rough stuff can miss a big climb and follow the Seixe valley through to **Odeceixe** (details below) but this is not a sensible option unless you're riding something reasonably rugged.

Extension/side trip

From Zambujeira, a 42km side trip takes you out to some of the most beautiful coastal scenery in the south-west Alentejo, including a dramatic headland and more gorgeous beaches.

For details see the entry listed in the **Day Rides** section under Zambujeira on page 192.

DIRECTIONS: MONCHIQUE – ZAMBUJEIRA

1. **(450m)** From the junction at the end of yesterday's stage, head north out of Monchique on the N266, climbing very gently until you come to a roundabout.

2. **(3.5km)** Go straight on, signposted 'Lisboa'. The N266 heads roughly north-east as it climbs then curves around to the north-west, with some wonderful views off to the right.

   Just past a couple of houses on the left, you'll come to a turning signposted 'Acaria do Peso' and 'Selão'.

3. **(2.8km)** Turn left here. The road turns west and continues until it meets (and becomes) the M501, which comes in from the left.

   Continue ahead on the M501. The road stays fairly level until it bends around to the right (north) at a junction where there's a turning signposted for Aljezur and Marmelete.

4. **(17.3km)** Stay on the M501 going north towards Selão. The road now enters a series of quite big bends, dropping around 260m over the next 6km as it heads north and then north-west towards a small settlement at the bottom of the valley.

   The descent then gets much more gradual as the M501 continues down into the Seixe valley. This is very wild country: there are a few small farms/settlements but most of it is just wooded hillsides.

   There's a basic café next to a left turn for Marmelete but nowhere else in particular to stop.

   Keep following the Seixe until you come to a right turn with a bridge over the river.

5. **(16.5km)** Turn right here (still on the M501). Over the next 2.2km the road climbs just over 200m as it heads north again – this section is the biggest climb of the day and contains the steepest incline (15%).

   After the worst of the climb, the road bends around to the right until its almost running south-east. There is a little more climbing to do on this section but it's nothing like as steep.

   Having passed through a large area of eucalyptus

plantation on the way up from the river, the road comes out into the open as it turns back to the north. The ride is mostly undulating for the next 5km, with some forested areas but also some open fields.

After a couple more bends, the road turns north-west and starts to descend steadily over the next 4km before levelling out.

At the end of about 3km of very gentle downhill you come to a junction with a road, signposted 'Sabóia', coming in from your right.

6. **(2km)** Keep straight on and you'll go up a small hill to a T-junction on the edge of São Teotónio (which has a confusing one-way system to negotiate).

7. **(200m)** Turn left and then right after 45m on a one-way street. Follow this around until you come to a five-way junction.

Note: The centre of town is more or less straight on from the left turn mentioned above. However, it's a bit of a maze to pick your way through and there's not a lot to see. Unless you're desperate for supplies it's probably easiest to keep going to Zambujeira.

8. **(800m)** Turn sharp right on what looks like a back street. The road bends around to the left and comes to a crossroads.

Go right here and continue until you come to a roundabout on the N120.

9. **(4.2km)** Go straight across the N120 onto the M502-1, signposted 'Cabo Sardão' and 'Casa Branca'.

Keep going until you come to a T-junction on a fairly flat plain with the sea just visible off to your left.

Note: You can continue to Cabo Sardão here or make a separate journey. To go direct to the cape, turn right then take the second turning on the left.

Otherwise see the Cabo Sardão day ride on page 192 for more information.

10. **(5.7km)** Turn left and follow the M502 for Zambujeira. There's a campsite to the left as you approach the village, while the centre of the village is straight ahead.

As you come into the centre of the village, the way ahead

is closed to traffic and the road bends to the right.

This is where the second stage ends. There are various **cafés**, **shops** and **restaurants** on the pedestrianised street ahead, which also leads to a clifftop area and the way down to a couple of spectacular **beaches**. (If you don't want to walk, turn right and then take the next left)

Alternative routes

1.

If you want to shorten the circuit and stick to the Algarve, one option is to go straight from Monchique to **Aljezur** (see page 58).

In this case, head south from Monchique (towards Caldas) on the N266 for about 2.7km and then turn right on to the N267.

This will take you all the way to Aljezur. It's also a beautiful ride, particularly the first part. Heading west, the road goes in and out around the contours for a while, before climbing to about 500m. It's then more or less downhill for the next 22km.

2.

As mentioned above, after descending along the M501 from Monchique you can continue along the Seixe valley for 14km to **Odeceixe**, which would also make a handy overnight stop before turning south (see **Second Night** details on page 49).

Beyond where the M501 crosses the river, the road along the valley (the M1002) is not flat and in January 2015 was in quite a bad state. It has a lot of dips and potholes and the surface has been badly chewed up by logging trucks.

The sealed road also turns left about 7km before Odeceixe and makes a big loop to the south, going up a huge hill. If you've made it this far on two wheels, there's a dirt road that follows the river. If dry, this will probably be no worse than the surface over which you've just ridden.

3. Sao Teotónio

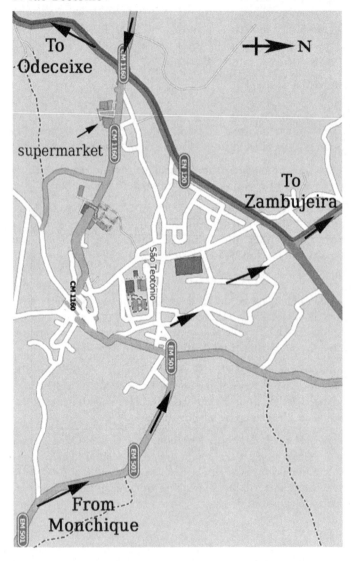

4. Zambujeira do Mar

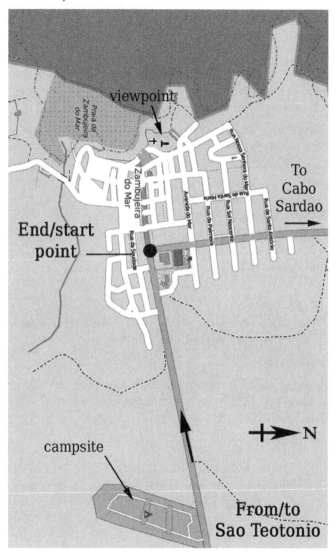

SECOND NIGHT

Zambujeira do Mar (pop 911) is an attractive small village, set on cliffs overlooking a pretty cove with a sheltered sandy beach.

Unlike resorts further north that attract mainly Portuguese visitors, Zambujeira tends to be more of a foreign backpacker hangout. It's popular with surfers, as well as anyone wanting a chilled-out winter sun bolthole.

In August the village is home to the **Sudoeste festival**, one of Portugal's biggest music events.

Headliners for 2015 include Calvin Harris, Emelie Sandé and Clean Bandit, while previous main acts have ranged from the Prodigy to Jamie Cullum and Daft Punk. (See: sudoeste.meo.pt/en)

Originally just a tiny fishing village, a few small villa developments have sprung up but it's still a low-key spot. Most of the restaurants and shops are along the pedestrian-only main street.

You're unlikely to be overwhelmed by the crowds but if you want to escape there are more sandy beaches the other side of headlands to the north and south of the village.

Supermarkets

There are a couple of mini-mercados in the village but no large shop. However, there is an **Intermarché** store in São Teotónio that's only just off the next day's route.

Accommodation

Camping:

There's a municipal site close to the village or a private one connected to a tourist resort and spa complex about 4.5km south (this can be accessed along a rough dirt road or by following the first stages of the ride for **Day Three**.)

Camping Zambujeira: a large site 400m from the village that also has apartments to rent.

Camping Zambujeira, 7630-740 Zambujeira do Mar.
Tel: 283 961 172 *Email:* campingzambujeira@gmail.com
Web: campingzambujeira.com
Price: €19. *Open:* April 1st – Oct 31st.

Monte Carvalhal da Rocha: set in farmland near some wild cliffs and small beaches, this site combines bungalows and a spa complex with camping.

Praia do Carvalhal, Brejão, 7630-569 Sao Teotónio.
Tel: 282 947 293 *Email:* geral@montecarvalhaldarocha.com
Web: montecarvalhaldarocha.com *Price:* €19.50.

Hotels & Guest Houses:

Residencial Mar-e-Sol, Rua Miramar 17 A, 7630-789 Zambujeira do Mar. *Tel:* 283 961 171
Email: r.maresol.zdm@gmail.com *Web:* maresol-residencial.com

Sol Dourado, Rua da Palmeira 43, 7630-794 Zambujeira do Mar.
Tel: 283 961 595 or 917 022 836
Email: soldouradozambujeira@gmail.com
Web: soldouradozambujeira.com

Alojamento Sudoeste, Avenida do Mar 47, 7630-785 Zambujeira do Mar. *Tel:* 919 207 577
Email: jesuszambujeira@gmail.com
Web: alojamentosudoeste.com

The Odemira tourist website also lists accommodation for Zambujeira – although it's not a comprehensive list. (Try a site like booking.com for other options.)
See: turismo.cm-odemira.pt

Odeceixe (pop 960) is an attractive small village set on the southern side of the Seixe valley, which forms the border between the Algarve and the Alentejo regions.

Just up from the riverside lies a compact centre of cobbled streets offering a choice of restaurants, shops, bars, guest houses etc..

Surrounding the village are some newer holiday flat developments, plus some older streets of more traditional, single-storey houses that climb up the hillside to the south.

A single windmill, painted in traditional style, overlooks the village centre.

The parish includes Praia de Odeceixe about 3km west of the main village. Here, a small hamlet overlooks a wide sandy beach at the mouth of the Seixe river. Just to the south of the main beach is a second cove, Praia de Adegas, which is one of Portugal's six official naturist (nudist) beaches.

Like Zambujeira to the north, Odeceixe is a bit of a hippy/surfer hangout. If you want to rent a board or learn how to catch a wave, there's a surf school at the beach.

Accommodation

Camping:

Camping São Miguel is technically in the Alentejo as it's up the hill on the other side of the river but it's only a stone's throw from Odeceixe. It's not that cheap but it looks like an attractive site with plenty of pine trees for shade.

Camping São Miguel,7630-592 São Teotónio.
Tel: 282 947 145 *Web:* campingsaomiguel.com

Hotels & Guest Houses:

Odeceixe Hostel, Rua das Amoreiras, 8670-320 Odeceixe, Portugal. *Tel:* 913 919 357

Residencia do Parque, Rua Estrada Nacional 15, 8670-320 Odeceixe. *Tel:* 282 947 117
Email: residenciadoparque-odeceixe@hotmail.com

Retiro do Adelinho, Rua Nova 20, 8670-320 Odeceixe.
Tel: 282 947 352

DAY THREE: ZAMBUJEIRA – ALJEZUR

Overview

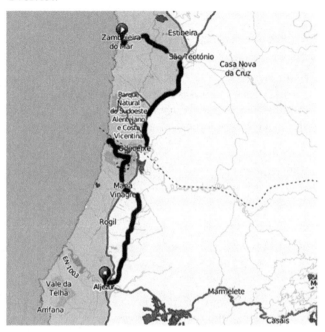

Today's stage takes you south, with a couple of opportunities to visit the beach (via sealed roads), including at Praia de Odeceixe, where there's a beautiful sandy bay that's very popular with surfers.

The rest of the time, though, you'll be riding inland as there is no coast road as such.

There are several other ways out to the cliffs and beaches but many of these are dirt tracks.

Otherwise, you're mainly riding through farmland and open countryside There are only a few hills and most of the cycling will be more or less on the flat.

There are two sections on the N120 (of about 9.2km total) which is the main road south. The road is generally relatively quiet but can get busy at peak season/weekends and is used by some trucks and larger vehicles.

Unfortunately, unless you're prepared to ride long sections on dirt tracks (see below for details), the N120 is the only option along this stretch of coast.

Apart from the two stretches on the main road, the rest of the route is almost entirely on minor back roads. Surfaces are a bit rough in places but at least you're more likely to meet a tractor than fast-moving cars or lorries.

Stats

Distance: 49.5km
Total elevation gain: +498m/-522
Maximum incline: 7.8%

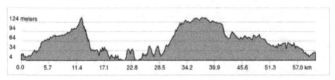

To download a map with full ride profile, available as .gpx file etc., see: ridewithgps.com/routes/7410236

Alternative routes

There is an alternative route for part of today's stage but this does involve some riding along dirt tracks that may get rough at times.

If you don't want to stop in Aljezur and intend riding all the way to **Sagres** (another 52.6km), it would be simple to cut today's stage to 35.1km by leaving out all the beach detours and simply sticking on the N120 from São Teotónio to south of Odeceixe, only leaving it at the turning for Carrascalinho (see **Point 8**).

Alternatively, you could cut the distance to about 40km by staying on the N120 until Odeceixe but still go out to the beach there.

Extension/side trips

There are a couple of options for rides from Aljezur to visit some of the other beautiful beaches on this stretch of coast.

- A 30km circuit out to Monte Clerigo and Arrifana involves a couple of tough climbs but is well worth it for the scenery.

- It's a shorter, there-and-back 14km ride to Praia da Amoreira. The road surface is rough but it's almost flat the whole way.

For details see page 146 in the **Day Rides** section.

DIRECTIONS: ZAMBUJEIRA – ALJEZUR

1. **(6.5km)** From the no-entry sign at the end of Zambujeira's pedestrianised main street, retrace your route back towards São Teotónio until you come to a right turn signposted 'Lagos'.

   Turn right and follow the M502-2 south-east (this road is also shown as the CM1160 on some maps). The road runs almost dead straight the whole way, rising gently as it heads away from the coast. Keep going until you come to a roundabout on the N120.

   Note: If you go straight ahead at the roundabout there's an Intermarché **supermarket** on the right after about 200m.

2. **(6.6km)** Turn right onto the N120 and follow the road southwards until you come to a right turn, signposted 'Azenha do Mar'. There's also a blue *parque de campismo* sign.

3. **(5.9km)** Turn right here and head north-west towards the hamlet of Brejão. Along the way you'll pass a gravel track that marks the end of the **alternative route**.

   Just past a small snack bar the road curves to the left and heads south-west and then south towards Azenha do Mar.

   Note: If you go straight on at the bend after the snack bar, it's a 6km round trip on a sealed road to another excellent sandy **beach** just beyond the Monte Carvalhal da Rocha holiday complex/**campsite**.

   The road south from Brejão brings you to the settlement of Azenha do Mar, set just back from a rocky cove that also houses a small but busy fishing harbour.

If you want to sample the local fish, there's a **restaurant** opposite the large parking area at the top of the cliffs.

4. **(5km)** You need to do a U-turn from Azenha do Mar. Follow the road back east for 500m and then north for another 500m.

Turn right on to an unmarked side road. Follow the road roughly south-east through an area of farmland covered with lots of polytunnels and crops growing under netting.

Follow the sealed road sharp left and then around a right-hand bend. Continue until you reach the N120.

5. **(2.6km)** Turn right on to the main road. It's downhill from here to Odeceixe – along the way passing the entrance to the **campsite** at Camping São Miguel.

The road curves to the right as it comes down into the Seixe valley and then turns left as it goes over the river.

6. **(3.6km)** Turn right immediately after the bridge

– there are brown beach signs for Odeceixe.

The streets in the centre are mostly cobbled. If you want to go into the village (which has a number of **cafés**, **bars**, **restaurants** and **shops**) the simplest option is to stop by the riverside after about 600m and walk up to your left.

Otherwise, keep following the river out to Praia de Odeceixe.

The road becomes a one-way system as you get closer to the beach and will bring you round to the top of a very steep street.

Note: You can walk down to the beach here or continue around a bit further and take the steps.

There are a couple of **cafés** (although these are closed in the winter), some **public toilets** and a **surf school** here.

7. **(8.3km)** Follow the one-way system around the clifftops, turn right at the roundabout and continue south-east and uphill.

The two-lane road becomes single-track and has a rougher surface as you head inland across farmland.

As you come back towards Odeceixe, there's a sharp right (signposted 'Lavajo') immediately before the road turns left at a small bridge over an irrigation channel.

Go right towards Lavajo and bear left at the next fork in the road, signposted 'Aljezur'.

8. **(11.2km)** Turn right when you reach the N120 and then, after about 200m, go left, signposted 'Carrascalinho'. The road takes you roughly east before curving to the south.

From here, it's a scenic, rural ride, mostly following a small valley, all the way to the edge of Aljezur. On the way, you pass the **campsite** at Quinta da Sombrinha (see **Third Night** on page 58).

The road climbs a little as it gets closer to the town and curves to the right.

Ignore the first right turn and take the second, which will take you straight down to a T-junction on the N120.

9. **(5.5km)** Turn left – going past the Intermarché **supermarket** – and then right at the roundabout. Follow the N120 over the bridge.

The main road turns left opposite a cobbled street and a café under a tall palm tree. This is where the third stage ends.

Alternative route

To avoid the first part of the N120, turn on to the M502-2 as described in **Point 1** above.

After 1.4km turn right again onto a small side road – the only signpost is likely to be a blue *turismo rural* sign. The road is sealed for about 3.9km, although quite rough in places.

The sealed surface runs out at a T-junction, where you turn right. Follow the track for 2.4km until you come to a sealed road going across your route.

Turn right and you are back on the main route – see **Point 3**.

MAPS: DAY THREE

5. Odeceixe

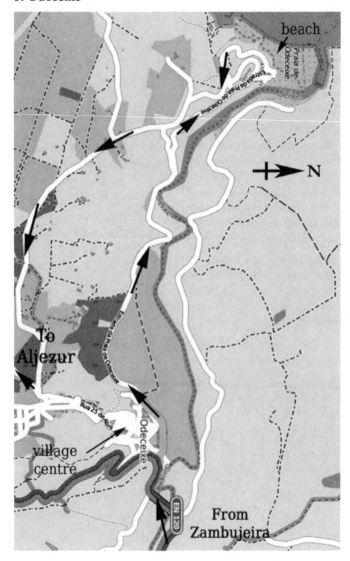

6. Aljezur

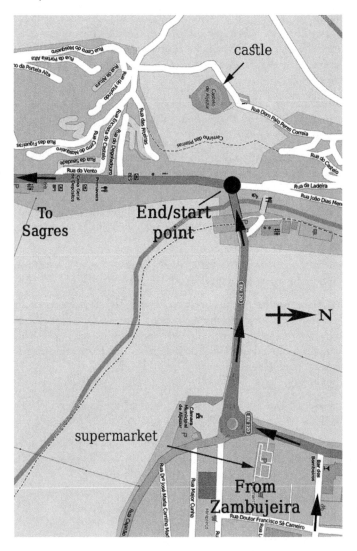

THIRD NIGHT

Aljezur (pop 5,900) is a pleasant but unremarkable town of two halves. On the eastern side of the Ribeira de Aljezur is a fairly nondescript modern town. Across the river is a much older network of narrow cobbled streets set on a steep hillside below a ruined castle.

Settlements in the area date back to the Stone Age, while Lusitanian tribes and the Romans also used the highpoint where the castle now stands.

However, like many places in the Algarve, the town itself was founded in the 10th century by the Muslim settlers from North Africa, who also built its castle.

Aljezur was captured from the Moors by the Portuguese in the mid-13th century – legend says a Moorish woman let the Christian knights into the citadel.

Although about 5km from the sea, Aljezur was once a small port with boats coming in to its riverside wharves.

The separation of Aljezur occurred in the 18th century when the population was urged to move across the river in a bid to escape from the malaria rife in the old town. However, only some inhabitants moved and – with malaria subsequently eradicated – the town remained divided.

The 1755 earthquake that flattened Lisbon also destroyed many houses in Aljezur and demolished most of the castle, which had already been abandoned for more than 300 years.

Although the largest town on the western coast of the Algarve, it's a quiet place. The old streets are worth a wander, as are the ruins of the castle, but there's not a lot of note to see.

Supermarkets

The **Intermarché** off the N120, in the new part of town, is the only shop of any size.

Accommodation

Camping:

There are two sites near the town, both a little way to the north and relatively expensive for Portugal.

Campismo do Serrão: set in countryside about 4km to the north of Aljezur and about 1km off the N120. Dirt tracks lead from the campsite to the beach at Praia da Amoreira.

Parque de Campismo do Serrão, Herdade do Serrão, 8670-121 Aljezur. *Tel:* 282 990 220 *Email:* info@campingserrao.com *Web:* campingserrao.com

Quinta da Sombrinha: small, ex-pat owned rural site with space for a few tents adjoining a holiday cottage.

Estrada do Carrascalinho, Saiceira, 8670-446 Rogil. *Tel:* 912 666 788 *Email:* quinta.da.sombrinha@sapo.pt *Web:* quinta-da-sombrinha.com

Youth hostel:

There's a new, smart-looking youth hostel out near the beach at Arrifana, about 9km from Aljezur.

To get to it, go south on the N120, turn right up a steep hill and left at the top. Follow the road to Arrifana. The hostel is in a modern, white building on the right.

Pousada de Juventude Arrifana, Urbanização Vale da Telha Lote 43/44 – Praia da Arrifana, 8670-111 Aljezur. *Tel:* 282 997 455 *Email:* arrifana@movijovem.pt *Web:* microsites.juventude.gov.pt/Portal/en/PArrifana.htm

Hotels & Guest Houses:

Amazigh Aljezur Hostel, Rua da Ladeira 5, 8670-065 Aljezur. *Tel:* 282 997 502 *Email:* booking@amazighostel.com *Web:* amazighostel.com

Carpe Vita, Rua Dr. César Viriato França, 8670-085 Aljezur. *Tel:* 963 256 581 *Email:* info@carpe-vita.com *Web:* carpe-vita.com

Vicente Aparthotel, Av. General Humber to Delgado, 8670-001 Aljezur.
Tel: 282 990 030 *Email:* geral@vicentina-aparthotel.com
Web: vicentina-aparthotel.com

For more options, including rural tourism properties in the surrounding area, see:
cm-aljezur.pt/externalPages/mapa_concelho/
default.aspx?lang=pt#/onde-dormir/estabelecimentos-hoteleiros

DAY FOUR: ALJEZUR – SAGRES

Overview

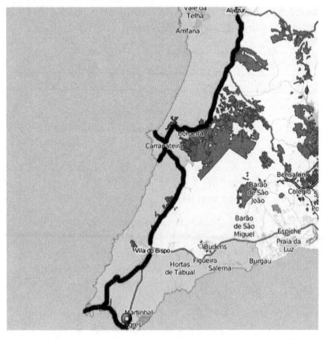

Today's stage is quite straightforward: a large part of it is on the N268 as there are no other options ride along this section of coast.

However, this is not generally a busy road except at peak holiday times and there are few HGVs on this stretch.

It's also very scenic. The majority of the riding is through a mixture of rural scenery and forest.

South of Aljezur the N268 runs several kilometres inland and there's no way out to the coast other than rough tracks.

After about 20km, though, the road turns west and brings you to the village of Carrapateira, which is not only a useful coffee/lunch top but is just inland from two of the most beautiful – and accessible – beaches on this stretch of coast.

Turning back inland again, there are a couple of reasonable hills (but no severe inclines) as the road climbs to a ridge before dropping down to Vila do Bispo.

From here, the landscape changes, becoming very open as you head out towards the wild and exposed headland at Sagres and Cabo São Vicente – the south–west tip of the European mainland.

Stats

Distance: 60.9km
Total elevation gain: +596m/-589
Maximum incline: 8.1%

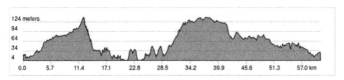

To download a map with full ride profile, available as .gpx file etc., see: ridewithgps.com/routes/7410294

Alternative routes

There are no alternative options on the section between Aljezur and Vila do Bispo if you're going to Sagres.

Between Vila do Bispo and Sagres you could take the main N268, which is part of the next day's route to Lagos. However, this means going further to get out to Cabo São Vicente, which is probably the biggest reason for coming here.

If you wanted to cut off Sagres completely (which would be a real shame), the N120 south of Aljezur takes a much more direct route to Lagos. This road is busier than the N268 and involves a long climb up from the coast but is mostly rural and very scenic.

DIRECTIONS: ALJEZUR – SAGRES

1. **(7.1km)** From the junction by the bridge over the Ribeira de Aljezur, head south on the N120 and continue past the turning for Arrifana.

   The road, which has a narrow shoulder, follows a gentle valley with fields to either side, and wooded hills beyond. It also climbs gently as it approaches a junction with the N268.

2. **(13.2km)** Turn right here, signposted 'V. Bispo' and 'Sagres' (brown sign). The road is narrower from here on with no shoulder but also less traffic.

   Continue, heading roughly south-south-west, climbing slightly as the N268 follows the valley. There are a few houses and small settlements along this stretch but it's mostly very rural and quiet.

   After coming up to the head of the valley, the road gets more undulating, with more bends, as it enters an area of forested hills. The road also descends as it turns west and passes the village of Bordeira off to the left.

   The N268 flattens out as it turns south again, with fields and sand dunes off to the right. Just after a small, white-painted bridge, you will come to a right turn, with a brown sign for the beach at Bordeira.

3. **(2.2km)** Turn right. There are several **cafés** and **restaurants** near here, including the wonderfully named Restaurante L-Colesterol, plus a couple of places advertising accommodation.

   As you approach an area of sand dunes there's a car park off to the right and you can see the sea. However, the only way to the beach from here involves wading across the river.

If you continue up the hill you'll come to a turning on the right for another car park. From here there's a path and steps down to Praia da Bordeira, which is a stunning beach and stretches north for about 3km (at low tide).

Again, the river lies between you and the beach but with the tide out it's an easy paddle.

4. **(2.8km)** Turn around at the car park and return to the N268 at Bordeira. Turn right and follow the road up and around to the left into Carrapateira.

    The centre of the village is off to the left. There are several **cafés**, as well as accommodation options and a small **mini-mercado**.

Note: It is possible to continue around the clifftops from the car park at Praia da Bordeira to the next beach at Praia do Amado but most of the track is unsealed.

This route is a bit rough in places but quite rideable, even on a loaded touring bike as long as you've got decent tyres.

The track will take you around some jagged cliffs and past a small fishing harbour before coming back onto a sealed road near a restaurant. It's then mostly downhill to another spectacular beach at Praia do Amado.

Taking this option only involves riding a few hundred metres further than having to backtrack between the two beaches and the N268.

5. **(2.2km)** Continue south from the village for about 250m and take the next right for Praia do Amado – the turning is a bit hidden by some large eucalyptus trees.

    The road is quite rough as it heads through some low, barren-looking hills. You'll come to two large car parks – sometimes full of parked camper vans. The beach, with a surf school and seasonal café, is just beyond.

6. **(14.5km)** Return to the N268 and turn south for Vila do Bispo. The road heads south-east into an area of wood and scrub-covered hills.

    After climbing gently to about 100m altitude, the road turns to the south again before coming out onto more open country near a turning for a village called Pedralva.

Continue south on the N268 from the Pedralva junction. The road is slightly rolling but more or less flat as it continues across an open, if windswept, hilltop plateau.

There's a nice downhill as you come towards Vila do Bispo, where there's a right turn into the centre just after the sign for the village.

7. **(800m)** Turn right and follow the road down, round a right-hand bend, and to a roundabout.

Turn left (second exit) and continue straight on to the next roundabout (with a sculpture of steel hoops). Take the second exit – towards the town's Lidl **supermarket**.

Note: If you need supplies, the centre of town lies in the area around the two roundabouts mentioned above and contains several other options apart from **Lidl**.

If you go straight on at the first roundabout, there's a market building just up the hill on your right. This contains a **mini-mercado** and several other shops.

Between the two roundabouts there are several **cafés** on the left. There was an Alisuper but this has now closed down.

8. **(9.7km)** Continue past Lidl. The road runs parallel with the main N268 for about 1.5km and then turns more to the south-west across open farmland.

After 5km the road does a 90° right turn. (The sealed surface does continue ahead but turns into a gravel track after about 200m).

Follow the road past a small white-painted house on the left and over a low rise. This will bring you to a T-junction on a gravel road.

Turn sharp left. The track continues south-west for about 1.6km to a collection of derelict-looking farm buildings.

Note: If you follow a track going off to the right (west) from the farm buildings for about 600m, it will take you to a wonderful, wild beach called Praia do Telheiro.

From the buildings, the track turns south and becomes sealed again, if a bit rough.

This will take you all the way

to a T-junction on the road out to Cabo São Vicente.

Note: As mentioned in **Point 8**, most of this section is sealed but – unless the road has been recently upgraded – it does involve about 1.6km of gravel track.

If you really don't want to ride on this, simply take the third exit from the roundabout on the southern side of Vila do Bispo and follow the N268 to Sagres.

Although this road can get quite busy at peak times, it's almost dead straight and has a wide shoulder for cycling on.

9. **(8.4km)** Turn right towards Cabo São Vicente. It's 2.3km out to the lighthouse across an almost completely flat headland, passing some spectacular cliffs to the left, as well as the remains of the Fortaleza de Belixe (destroyed by Sir Francis Drake in 1570 and abandoned after the 1755 earthquake).

The views from around the lighthouse are stunning – particularly around sunset. Look out for the local fishermen, perched on the edge of the cliffs as they lower their lines around 60-70m to the sea.

From the cape, simply retrace your steps and follow the road straight on for Sagres. Go past the popular surfing beach at Beliche and straight across at the first roundabout (second exit).

You pass an Alisuper **supermarket** on the left and the next roundabout marks the western end of the main street and the end of the day's stage.

MAPS: DAY FOUR

7. Carrapateira & Bordeira

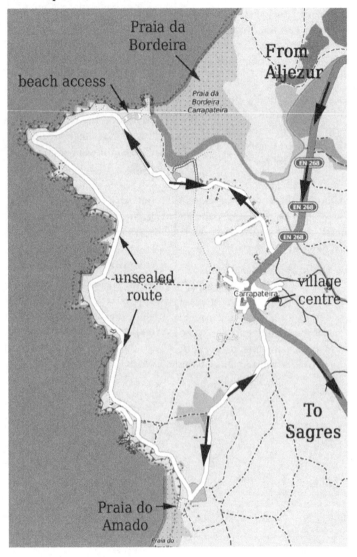

8. Vila do Bispo

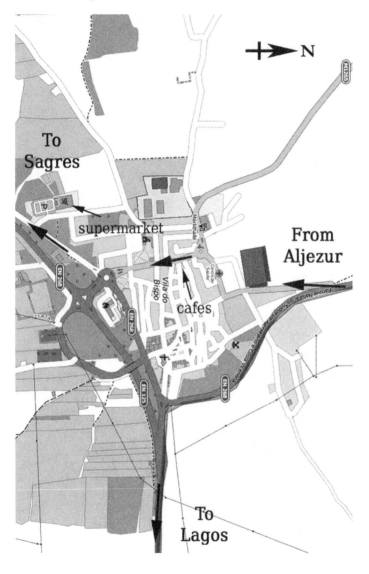

9. Cabo São Vicente

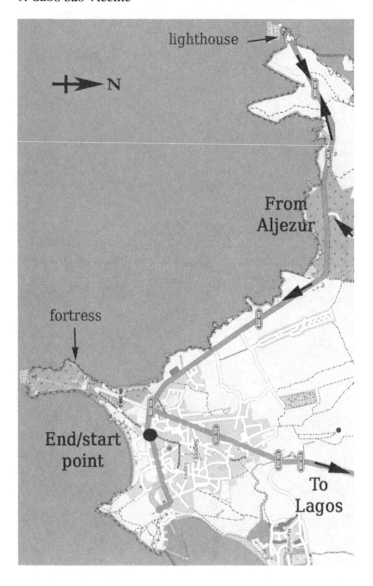

10. Sagres

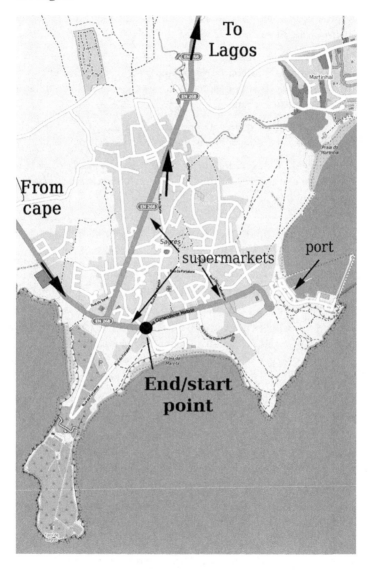

FOURTH NIGHT

Sagres (pop 1,900) has an 'end of the world' feel. The only road of any size – in and out – comes from Vila do Bispo, 9km away.

North of Sagres, the landscape is almost bare of trees and a mixture of gently rolling farmland and wild scrubland stretches to the horizon. To the west, south and east there's only one thing to see: the Atlantic Ocean.

The name Sagres comes from *sagrado*, meaning 'holy' and the headland was once regarded as the end of the known world.

Although there was a mediaeval village here, the location came to prominence in the 15th century when Prince Henry the Navigator began building a fortified town – the *Fortaleza* – on a flat headland.

Henry was the third son of Portugal's King John I (*João I*) and owned a lot of land and fisheries in the Algarve.

He is also widely credited with having launched the Age of Discoveries that led to Portugal becoming one of the world's seapowers.

Legend has it that Henry set up a 'school of navigation' at Sagres but, while he did employ a number of mapmakers there, most voyages sponsored by the *Infante* prince set off from Lagos.

As well as exploring the west coast of Africa, Henry's navigators also sailed further out into the Atlantic than ever before, discovering the Madeira and Azores islands, which were soon settled by the Portuguese.

These days, the main attraction for many visitors is the superb local surfing – helped by having access to beaches pointing in various directions.

Divers and boat trips to see whales, dolphins and other marine wildlife also set off from the town's busy fishing harbour.

Sagres is a lowrise, sprawling place with no real centre. It's not exactly pretty but it's got a definite charm, with lots of clifftops and beaches to explore.

Supermarkets

There a large, modern **Intermarché** store about 1km from the town centre. It's just off the N268 heading north out of town, on the right-hand side.

The town also has two fair sized branches of **Alisuper**. One is midway along the main street (Rua Comandante Matoso), the other is on the way into town coming from the cape.

Accommodation

Camping:

Campsite Orbitur Sagres is just over 2km out to the north of town. It's fairly expensive but open all year and set in a wooded, rural location.

Cerro das Moitas, 8650-998 Sagres.
Tel: 282 624 371 *Web:* orbitur.com/campsite-orbitur-sagres

Hotels & Guest Houses:

Casa Grilo, Rua Pedra da Bala, 8650 – 386 Sagres
Tel: 913 614 094 *Email:* casagrilosagres@hotmail.com
Web: facebook.com/casagrilosagres/info

Hotel Apartment Don Tenorio (3*), Rua do Norte, 8650-365 Sagres.
Tel: 282 624 364/6 *Email:* dontenorioaparthotel@hotmail.com
Web: dontenorioaparthotel.web.pt

Residencia Júlio, Rua da Marreira – Apartado 6, 8650-232 Sagres. *Tel:* 282 624 448 *Email:* info@residenciajulio.com
Web: residenciajulio.com

For other options, including lots of *quartos* (rooms) in family homes, and accommodation in Vila do Bispo and surrounding villages, see:

cm-viladobispo.pt/pt/menu/95/onde-dormir.aspx*

*choose between:
- *alojamento local* (rooms in Guest Houses and private homes)
- *empreendimentos turísticos* (hotels and holiday complexes)

DAY FIVE: SAGRES – LAGOS

Overview

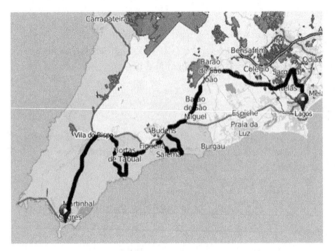

This stage takes you back east on a somewhat zigzag route that visits more lovely beaches and some quiet country lanes.

Initially you have to return to Vila do Bispo and take the N125 for a short distance. After that, you take some tiny lanes that are unmarked on most maps, following small valleys down to the coast and then back inland.

Some of today's ride follows the same route as the Ecovia do Litoral, a long-distance cycle route that (theoretically) runs from Sagres to the Spanish border. The Ecovia is extremely poorly marked though, so don't rely on its signposts. (It also goes off onto some rough gravel tracks in places.)

After the fourth beach at Boca do Rio, your route turns inland, avoiding a couple of the more built-up resorts just to the west of Lagos. There is another short stretch on the N125, after which you ride north-east on a country road towards a couple of villages.

You then turn more south-east across some low hills and farmland before a last zigzag to come in to Lagos from the east. The last section into town is fairly busy but it's better than coming in from the west, which involves riding through busy, built-up areas for longer.

Stats

Distance: 54.7km
Total elevation gain: +711m/-736
Maximum incline: 9.8%

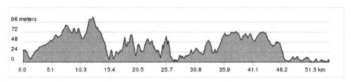

To download a map with full ride profile, available as .gpx file etc., see: ridewithgps.com/routes/7410418

Alternative routes

One option if you're in a hurry is simply to follow the N125 from Vila do Bispo all the way to Lagos, which cuts the distance to 34km.

The N125 can get busy – particularly in peak season and as you get closer to Lagos – but it's not too bad for cycling. There is a wide shoulder along nearly all the N125 and it's mostly still quite scenic.

Extension/side trips

There are several options for rides from Lagos to explore some of the surrounding countryside and visit some of the beaches out to the west. These include:

- A 32.7km ride up to the Barragem da Bravura reservoir
- Two rides of 16.4km and 6km from the station at Mexilhoeira Grande (a short train trip from Lagos

For details see Lagos (page 163) and Mexilhoeira (page 176) in the **Day Rides** section.

DIRECTIONS: SAGRES – LAGOS

1. **(1.1km)** From the roundabout where the previous stage ended, go north on Rua do Mercado – signposted *'centro do saude'*, *'mercado municipal'* and *'igreja'*.

   Go straight on at the next roundabout. After just over 100m, take a road going off to the left at an angle – there should be a blue sign for a hotel.

   The lane you're on comes to a T-junction. Turn left and then after only about 25m you come to another T-junction.

2. **(9.7km)** Turn right on to the N268, which is the main road out of town.

   The road takes you back north across a very open, quite barren-looking plateau to Vila do Bispo, where the N268 joins with, and becomes, the N125.

   A couple of minor ups and downs follow and then the N125 comes to the village of Raposeira, where there is a set of traffic lights in the centre.

   Note: there are a couple of **cafés** on the other side of the N125 at Raposeira, plus one on the left just after you turn off at the lights.

3. **(1.1km)** Turn right at the traffic lights – there are brown signs for beaches at Ingrina and Zavial.

   You soon leave the village. Follow the road roughly south-east and out into the countryside. The landscape here is quite different from the open plateau near Sagres, with lots of small hills and a much more undulating road.

   Coming up to the top of a hill, you reach a staggered crossroads.

4. **(6.3km)** Turn right here, following the brown sign for Ingrina. The road climbs to an altitude of 100m and you're on top of the world (well, this bit of it).

   A brown tourism sign indicates some *megaliticos* (megaliths) just off the road.

   Continue south and downwards. Most of the landscape here is open hillside, covered by low scrub. Then a couple of streetlights and a row of incongrous palm trees announce a small complex of tourist apartments seemingly plonked in the middle of nowhere.

Carry on down to Ingrina, one of many popular over-wintering spots for camper vans along this stretch of coast. The beach here is only small and disappears at hightide, leaving just a rocky cove.

From Ingrina there's a short uphill and then a steep descent to the popular surfing spot of Zavial. Again, there's little sand at high tide but if the water is low, a large and gorgeous beach appears around the corner to the left.

The road goes left and north from Zavial, following a small valley up to Hortas do Tabual.

5. **(3.2km)** Turn right in Hortas – following the sign for the village. You're now on a one-lane road that winds up and down through more fields and scrubby hills.

6. **(3.2km)**The road comes to a T-junction just outside the village of Figueira. Turn right here and towards the village – there's a **café** tucked away just off to the left. (There's also a new campsite but at present it appears to only be for campervans.)

Continue up past the village and go straight on, back towards the N125. Literally a few metres before the roundabout on the main road, there's a turning right, signposted 'Salema'.

Turn right here and the road takes you down into a narrow, quite deep valley. Along the way, you pass a year-round **campsite** on the right. Continue straight on as you enter Salema.

There's a small plaza with several **café/restaurants** and a small Alisuper **supermarket**, plus places offering accommodation. The beach is just beyond the small car park area.

7. **(2.5km)** Backtrack from the beach and turn right to continue along the road that brought you down to Salema.

The road climbs steadily as it loops around the village. At the top of the hill, you can fork off to the right to continue to the next beach but most of this is gravel.

Otherwise, follow the road to the left and then take a sharp right at the bottom to ride out to the beach at **Boca do Rio** (see page 78).

8. **(5.2km)** Retrace your steps from Boca do Rio, going past the road you came down on from Salema and continue north up the valley.

A lovely rural road brings you up to the N125 just outside the village of Budens.

Turn right on the N125 (there's an Intermarché **supermarket** opposite) and continue for 2.2km to the second set of traffic lights after Budens.

In order to turn left, you need to go right, signposted 'Bensafrim', 'Barão S. Miguel' and 'Barão S. João', and cross the N125 at the lights on to the M535.

9. **(6.3km)** From the traffic lights, the road goes up over some low, scrubby hills and then down into farmland, heading north-east towards the first village of Barão de São Miguel. There's a **café** on a corner on your left but not much else to see.

The M535 turns more to the north, climbing slightly. It continues across a landscape of open fields and occasional patches of scrub to Barão de São João, a larger and more interesting village.

Keep straight on until you come to a T-junction, where the main road curves around to the right, signposted 'Lagos'. The centre of Barão de São João is to the left, containing several **cafés** and a cobbled main street leading off a small square by the church.

10. **(9.7km)** Go right towards Lagos. The road becomes the M535-1 and turns south-east for about 8km.

It's an undulating road but without any big hills, going past a few small farms and a lot of semi-wild looking fields and scrub-covered slopes.

The M535-1 crosses a motorway on a small bridge, climbs a bit of a rise and gives you a nice downhill to a T-junction on the N120.

Turn left (away from Lagos) and take the next right in about 150m. The lane zigzags around as it crosses a small river (the Ribeira de Bensafrim) and heads across fields to the village of Caldeiroa, bringing you to a junction on a steep bend opposite a café.

Note: You can turn right on the N120 for a more direct route to Lagos. However, there's a fairly steep hill going this way – plus a fairly narrow section on a bend with no hard shoulder.

This section of road can be busy with local traffic at times, often going quite fast, and the route suggested below is probably quite a bit safer.

11. **(4.7km)** Go straight ahead (back on to the M535-1). In about 500m the road turns sharp right, becoming Estrada do Paúl.

The road now runs south for about 2.4km to a T-junction on the N125 just outside Lagos.

Turn right here – this road is normally busy but there's a wide shoulder all the way to the edge of town.

Unfortunately the shoulder runs out (and is replaced with a pavement) just before the bridge over the Ribeira de Bensafrim estuary. However, the road is straight and visibility is good so you should be safe.

Note: An alternative and quieter route into the town centre from that described in **Point 12** is to go left at the junction just before the bridge.

It's not legal to turn left here so you will need to walk across – watching carefully as the traffic can be very busy at times.

Once across, rejoin the road opposite the Pingo Doce **supermarket** car park. At the next junction follow the road left, signposted 'Meia Praia'. Keep going past some apartment blocks to the next roundabout.

Turn right and follow the road around the back of the pink Marina de Lagos building. You'll see the train station ahead and to your left. Keep going to the right, and you'll come to a pedestrian bridge over the river.

Cross here to emerge on the town's riverside promenade a few hundred metres north of the end point described below.

12. **(1.7km)** Once over the river on the N125, turn left at the next roundabout once you're over the river. Follow the dual carriageway past McDonald's. Keep following

the N125 as it curves around to the south.

At the next roundabout (with the ship water feature in the middle) take the third exit, signposted '*centro*'.

Go straight on at the next roundabout – still on the N125 – and as the road curves to the right you come on to the town's riverside with a wide promenade to your left.

You'll also see the marina through the palm trees that line the length of the riverside.

Keep going past the bus station on your right and the first of the shops and cafés. The town's market is in a white building on the right and then you come to a grassy island in the middle of the road.

Off to the right is a pedestrianised shopping area leading off into the old town. This is the end of the day's stage.

Boca do Rio

Like many beaches along this part of the coast, much of Praia da Boca do Rio disappears when the tide is in. At low tide, however, it's another matter with getting on for 2km of golden sand stretching off to the left.

It's also a lovely walk along the sand from Boca do Rio to the next beach at Cabanhas Velhas and the ruined harbour on the headland beyond.

Watch out for the cliffs, though. They are high and fairly unstable, as can be seen from the number (and size) of boulders littering the beach. At low tide you can walk a fair way from the cliffs but it can be a more unnerving, if not to say dangerous, when the tide is further in.

You can also see the ruins of the **Forte de Almádena** perched right on the edge of the cliffs close to Boca do Rio. There's not much left of the fort and it's a steep climb up the road from the beach but the views are magnificent.

MAPS: DAY FIVE

11. Lagos area

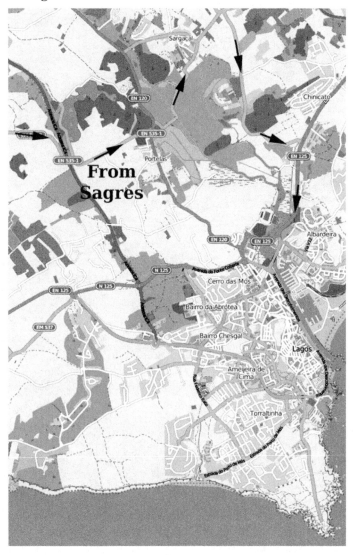

12. Lagos centre

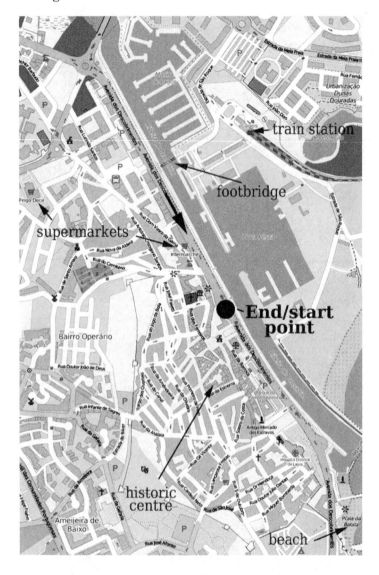

FIFTH NIGHT

Lagos (pop 22,000) is best known these days as an attractive riverside town to the west of the region's main resort area.

Once upon a time, though, Lagos was the Algarve's rich and powerful capital: the base for Portuguese navigators who sailed into the great unknown as they launched the country's Age of Discoveries.

Originally settled by Iberian tribes, *Lacobriga* was home to the Carthiginians, Romans, Visigoths and Byzantines before the Moors took control in the 8th century and built Lagos's castle.

In 1174 the Muslim rulers allowed local Christians to build a church to St John the Baptist just outside the walls – making it the oldest church in the Algarve.

The city remained in Moorish hands until the middle of the 13th century when the Christian forces of the Portuguese captured Lagos.

In less than two centuries the city became the centre of Portuguese maritime power; its explorers led the way in opening up the African continent to European traders and raiders.

The goods and riches that flowed to Lagos included many captured Africans and the city soon became the centre of Europe's new slave trade.

Lagos remained an important and prosperous city until 1755, when the old city was destroyed in a huge earthquake and subsequent tsunami. Although Lagos never regained its former glory, it remains one of the top destinations on the Algarve coast.

A sprawl of modern development surrounds the historic centre but it's not as overwhelming or characterless as the miles of holiday villas that have swamped some former seaside villages further east.

The old town – which also has most of the restaurants, shops, bars and nightclubs – lies on the west bank of the Ribeira de Bensafrim, opposite a fishing harbour and modern marina.

Sections of its old walls ring a network of cobbled streets that radiate out from a pedestrianised heart.

Although Lagos itself lies on the river, there are some fabulous beaches all around the town. To the east, just across the rivermouth, is the long expanse of Meia Praia.

Immediately south, a line of crumbling cliffs and eroded stacks is dotted with a series of golden coves. This leads a couple of kilometres to the Ponta de Piedade (*Piety Point*) where a lighthouse stands above steps leading down to some small sea caves.

West of the town, the cliffs continue above more golden sands at Praia de Canavial, which leads to another beautiful beach at Porto de Mós.

Supermarkets

Lagos has branches of most of Portugal's chains. The most convenient, however, are probably a smallish **Intermarché** on the riverfront just north of the town's market (open Mon-Sat), and new **Pingo Doce** and **Lidl** stores a short way to the north-east.

There's another **Pingo** on the way into town to the north of the marina, plus a big **Continenté** up the hill to the north of town and a large **Intermarché** on the N125 coming in from the west.

Bike Shops

Xtreme Bikes is a Specialized stockist, up the hill a little from the centre of town at Rua da Gafaria, Lote 11.

Tel: 282 760 978. *Email:* xtremelagos@gmail.com

Accommodation

Camping:

There's only one campsite open to the public in Lagos but several other sites in the local area – although be warned that prices are a lot higher around here than in the less touristy parts of Portugal.

Camping Trinidade is listed as a one-star campsite but is also the only one in Lagos open to the public. Compact site on the southern edge of town.

Rossio da Trindade, 8600-906 Lagos.
Tel: 282 763 893. *Email:* campismotrindade@gmail.com
Web: campingtrindade.pt.la *Price:* €12.00 *Open:* All year.

Note: There's an attractive-looking site in a great position just off the N125 as it curves around the southern side of the town centre. However, this is a 'military only' facility for soldiers and their families.

Orbitur Valverde is little way inland from the resort village and beach at Praia da Luz.

Estrada da Praia da Luz,8600-148 Lagos.
Tel: 282 789 211. *Web:* orbitur.com/campsite-orbitur-valverde
Price: €20.40. *Open:* All year.

Turiscampo is a pleasant-looking site just off the main road to Sagres, next to the village of Espiche and about 5km from Lagos (but with a bus stop outside).

Estrada Nacional 125, 8600-109 Lagos.
Tel: 282 789 265. *Email:* info@turiscampo.com
Web: turiscampo.com/en/ *Price:* €18 low season to €34 in high

Quinta dos Carriços lies in a shady site in a valley just above the old fishing village and pretty beach at Salema.

Praia da Salema, 8650-196 Budens.
Tel: 282 695 201 *Email:* quintacarrico@gmail.com
Web: quintadoscarricos.com/en/index.html *Price:* €18. *Open:* All year.

Chickenrun Campsite is a small rural site owned by English ex-pats near the village of Mexilhoeira Grande.

Casa Chickenrun, Varzia do Farelo, Mexilhoeira Grande, 8500-160 Portimão.
Tel: +44 792 323 5757 *Email:* chickenrun_info@aim.com
Web: andleycamping.com/index.html *Price:* €5 *Open:* All year.

Hotel Marina Rio (4), Av. dos Descobrimentos, 8600-645 Lagos.
Tel: 282 780 830 *Email:* marinario@net.vodafone.pt
Web: marinario.com/en/marina-rio-hotel.html

Casa a Sul, Rua da Atalaia 18, 8600-686 Lagos.

Casinha Algarvia, Praça João de Deus 12 (Praça D'Armas), 8600-523 Lagos.

Dina's Guesthouse, Travessa do Mineiro 1, 8600-634 Lagos.
Tel: 969 887 514

Unfortunately, I've never been able to find a single website listing the many accommodation options in Lagos. I would suggest a site like booking.com to check what's available.

DAY SIX: LAGOS – SILVES

Overview

This could be the toughest day of the circuit. At 73.5km it's the longest in terms of distance and involves another big ascent, from sea level to around 440m (1,450ft) – see below for the 44km **alternative route**.

The main route takes you out past the Meia Praia beach before turning north and inland, past Odiaxere and into quiet countryside as it heads into the hills above the large Barragem da Bravura reservoir.

There are a couple of warm up climbs in the first 24km but most of the riding is pretty gentle, much of it following small valleys.

Leaving the reservoir behind, you'll need your low gears for one section. However, while there are a couple of steep spots, the average gradient on the main hill only works out at about 6%.

After turning towards Marmelete, there's a bit more climbing to do but beyond the village the road is so smooth and the gradient so gentle you'll hardly notice it unless you've got a head wind (unlikely going east).

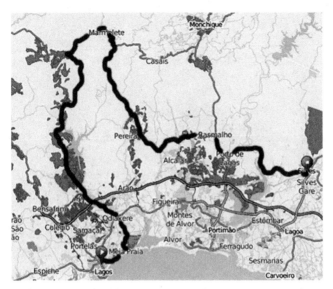

Turning south, you drop back off the hill and around some serious bends that will test your brakes. It's all very rural and quite wild in places...until you suddenly come across the Algarve International Autodrome (see page 93), a €195m race track used for Formula One testing and all kinds of motorsports events.

It's a somewhat surreal sight after the wilds of the surrounding countryside and once past, you're soon back on quiet rural roads. There are a few more ups and downs but nothing major and it's all very scenic.

The route joins the N266 south of Caldas de Monchique and then takes the N124 to Silves, the final 10km returning along the same section as when leaving town at the start of the circuit.

From Silves, you can follow the **Loulé Connection** (see page 96) if you want to extend your tour.

Stats

Distance: 73.5km
Total elevation gain: +1176m/-1169
Maximum incline: 14.7%

To download a map with full ride profiles, available as .gpx file etc., see: ridewithgps.com/routes/7438824

Alternative routes

If the above option seems too daunting, there is a much easier, 44km alternative that only involves small hills (with a total ascent of less than half that of the main route).

This route mainly follows some very pleasant and quiet country lanes taking you north-east from Odiaxere before rejoining the main route just south of the autodrome.

Extension/side trips

If you want to explore the hills to the north-east of Silves, a 59.5km circuit takes you out to the Arade and Funcho reservoirs and the small town of São Bartolomeu de Messines before looping back through the countryside to the east of your start point.

This ride can also easily be reduced to just over 46km by ending the ride at Alcantarilha (the station for Armacão de Pêra) and catching the train back to Silves.

For details see the entry under Silves (page 184) in the **Day Rides** section.

DIRECTIONS: LAGOS – SILVES

1. **(1km)** The ride starts where the previous day's stage ended: on the riverside opposite the pedestrianised shopping area in the centre of the old town.

   Head back upriver and after 450m take the footbridge that crosses over to the marina. Go straight ahead and follow the road around the back of the marina building until you come to a roundabout.

2. **(2.5km)** Turn right and follow the road (across one roundabout) past various apartment developments towards Meia Praia. There are two annoying sections of cobbles but luckily neither is that long.

   The road runs parallel with the beach, about 200m inland, bringing you to a roundabout near the Meia Praia train station.

3. **(4.6km)** Turn left and follow the road up the hill. It's a steady climb but not too far to a T-junction at the top. Turn right here towards the golf club and then left and downhill.

   There's another T-junction at the bottom. Go right and then take the next left, which will bring you into the village of Odiaxere.

   The road curves to the right as it drops down and crosses a small valley just before the village. There's then a short, sharp hill as the road bends back to the left, bringing you up to a small plaza by the church and the main N125.

4. **(5.5km)** Turn left on the N125 and then right in 120m, just after the traffic lights at a pedestrian crossing.

   Go straight on north, past the village market on the left. As you leave the village there's a wide plaza on the right with a renovated traditional windmill.

   The road dips down and curves to the left, signposted '*Barragem*' (dam/reservoir). You're soon in countryside, following a shallow valley with a few farms and small groups of houses dotted around the fields.

   Continue north-west under the A22 motorway. Just past a hamlet called Cotifo, there's a fork in the road.

5. **(9.8km)** Go left here, signposted 'Marmalete', 'Aljezur', and 'Monchique'. The road starts to climb a little as it goes up towards the reservoir but it's all relatively gentle.

The scenery gets wilder from here, with fewer farms and fields, and the hills getting closer and more rugged. After about 4km and a climb of about 60m, the road briefly runs along the edge of the reservoir.

The first real hill of the day follows as you head up into an area of eucalyptus plantation. There are some great views from the top – unfortunately there's also a downhill to follow that means you lose all of the height just gained.

There's a junction near the head of the reservoir – go right and keep following signs for Marmelete. More gentle climbing follows, which continues until you reach a turning for a track to Três Figos (*Three Figs*).

6. **(7.4km)** The road bends to the right as it goes up and over another steep but fairly short hill. On the other side it curves back north.

As you come down past the sign for Romeiras there's a basic **café** on your left and then another on the right about 500m further on.

7. **(6.8km)** Turn right on the N267. Running along a wooded ridge, the views to left and right give you a real sense of how high you've climbed – at this point an altitude of around 350m above sea level.

From the second café, Casa Pacheco, the road continues gently for a short distance then bends left and starts to go up more steadily.

This is the start of the biggest climb of the day. The main part ascends around 170m over 2.6km – giving an average gradient of 6.5%.

After you get to the top of the climb, the road dips down and then back up again to come to a T-junction on the N267 that runs between Aljezur and Monchique.

The road goes up and down for the next 6.3km as it follows the ridge around to Marmelete.

Note: You can turn off right just before the village to take a back way in – look for the brown '*zona historica*' sign. Although quite pretty, much of this route is cobbled.

As you come into Marmelete on the N267 the road curves to the south. There are a couple of **cafés** and one **snack bar/restaurant** just off the main road.

The village lies at just below 400m and the road continues to climb as it heads south but only very gently and it's only 1.5km to a right turn, signposted 'Corte Cibrão' and 'Folga'.

Note: If you don't mind a bit more gentle climbing and are enjoying the views, it's about 3.2km further from this junction to the high point on the N267. It's also a very pleasant ride, with the road curving through woodland around some gentle bends.

There's a bus stop on a wide bend at a place called Portela do Vale where the road reaches a height of 500m (1,640ft) with some stunning views down to the coast when the air is clear.

8. **(9.5km)** Turn right towards Folga – and keep your hands on your brakes. The road drops around 230m over the next 2.1km, with an average gradient of about 11% and up to 14% in places.

It's also a single-track road and the surface is a bit uneven in places as it descends through eucalyptus forest to a tight right-hand bend at the top of a small valley.

There are a few tatty agricultural buildings and scattered small farms but not much else out here. The road continues to descend, although much more gently, as you head south past some overgrown terraces.

After a long run south, almost all of it downhill, it's a bit of a shock when you come to a small uphill section about 9km after turning off the N267.

But the hill isn't anything like as big a surprise as what lies over the top: a smooth, two-lane road that takes you under a flyover and brings you down to a roundabout just outside an international motorsports circuit! (For more information on the **Algarve International Autodrome** see page 93).

9. **(7.1km)** Turn right at the first roundabout. Follow the

road around the outside of the autodrome, going straight on at the next roundabout.

At the third roundabout take the third exit, signposted 'Alcalar'. From here you're back onto quiet country roads for the next section, following an undulating route, roughly south-east until you come to a staggered crossroads.

Turn left here and continue north-east for 1.5km until you come to a T-junction.

Turn right and then, after 500m, go right again on to the M532. Keep going to the next left turn.

10. **(4.9km)** Turn left here — there are lots of signs for the other directions but the only one indicating the way you want to go is for an *escola primaria* (primary school).

It's not quite so wild around here. The landscape is more open, with quite a few more houses to be seen.

After about 800m there's a slight downhill and you turn right at the next junction. From here, follow the road roughly east for just over 4km until you come to a T-junction on the N266.

11. **(14.4km)** Turn right onto the N266 Portimão-Monchique road. This road can be busy at times but it's straight, and visibility is good.

After 2.5km, you reach a roundabout. Go left here (second exit) on the N124 towards Silves. The surface on this road is a lot rougher in places but it generally gets a lot less traffic.

There's a bit of a climb as you go up through some scrubby hills before going back down into the Odelouca valley.

Where you cross the river on the N124 you rejoin the original route out from Silves at the start of day one of the circuit and it's another 9.7km back to the town.

Follow the road around the southern side of Silves to finish the **Touring Circuit** at the same spot by the old bridge. (Alternatively, bear left as you approach town to go up into the historic centre.)

Note: See page 28 for notes on accommodation etc. in Silves.

Alternative route

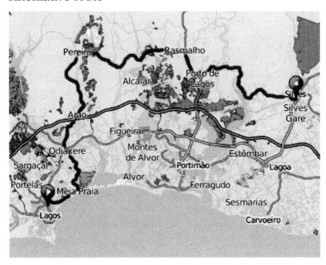

As mentioned above, the beginning and end for this option are the same as for the longer route. The big difference is that you miss out the big climb up to Marmelete.

This alternative middle section is all on quiet lanes and country back roads where you're unlikely to encounter much traffic. It's not flat but overall it's a lot more gentle.

Stats

Distance: 44km
Total elevation gain: +508m/-502
Maximum incline: 7.2%

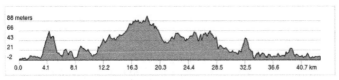

To download a map with full ride profiles, available as .gpx file etc., see: ridewithgps.com/routes/7438894

DIRECTIONS: LAGOS – SILVES (ALTERNATIVE ROUTE)

To start with, head along Meia Praia beach and to Odiaxere as described in **Points 1-3** for the main route (see page 87).

After passing the windmill in **Point 4** – about 350m from the N125 – there is a side turning on the right where the road dips down and curves to the left. Follow these directions from this point:

1. **(2.7km)** Turn right, signposted 'Alfarrobeira' and 'Arão'. Follow the road across some fields and up a gentle hill past a few houses. Turn right at the first T-junction then immediately left. This will bring you to another junction almost beneath a motorway flyover.

2. **(6.9km)** Turn left on the M539 to go under the A22 motorway. The road heads north through farmland and, after about 500m, turns right over a small bridge, joining the M1068.

   Go straight ahead onto the M1068 as you cross the bridge, signposted 'Montes de Cima' and 'Pereira'.

   The single-lane road continues north-east, climbing gently. It then turns north and drops into a slightly wilder valley with some abandoned fields and wooded hills to either side.

Note: Unless the council has finally got around to doing some work, you may see a large warning sign with the message: '*Atenção! Pavimento em mau estado. Depressões no pavimento.*'

This translates as: 'Attention. Surface in bad condition. Subsidence in the road.'

The next few kilometres have some very uneven sections. The surface is mostly intact – just don't try riding with no hands while admiring the view!

You'll come back into more populated farmland. There are a few small houses next to the road as you approach the hamlet of Pereira. There are two **cafés** here, one where the road bends to the left and then another opposite a right turn.

3. **(1.6km)** Turn right here, signposted Portimão.

   This road brings you to a roundabout just to the south of the autodrome (see following page) – turn left here if you want to take a look at the racetrack.

Otherwise, this is the third roundabout described in **Point 9** of the directions for the main route. Go straight ahead (second exit) to continue along the M1145, signposted 'Alcalar'.

Follow the remaining directions for the main route, starting at the second paragraph of **Point 9** (page 90).

Autódromo Internacional do Algarve

The Algarve autodrome, also known as the Portimão Circuit, was completed in 2008 at a cost of €195 million.

After being approved by the world governing bodies for both four and two-wheel motor-racing, the first event held there was a final round of the 2008 Superbike World Championship. Since 2010 it's been used for Formula One testing and has hosted a number of events featuring different motorsports.

The project was the brainchild of local entrepreneur and racing fanatic Paulo Pinheiro, who spent seven years on the project. Unfortunately, the circuit has never recouped its costs. It was taken over by a state-owned venture capital company in 2013, with reports that Pinheiro's company had debts of €160 million.

Although large events still take place fairly regularly, it's not entirely surprising the 4.7km circuit is not making much money. According to locals, races are poorly marketed and promoted, and there's an over-complex system for buying tickets – which doesn't always work.

It's also an extremely bizarre sight for anyone cycling down out of the hills. Set among scrub-covered hills, the racetrack, associated karting circuit, stands, car parks etc. cover around 300 hectares.

Suddenly coming across the autodrome feels like being transported to another world. Loop around it and cross the link road to the motorway, though, and you're soon back in peaceful countryside.

13. Meia Praia

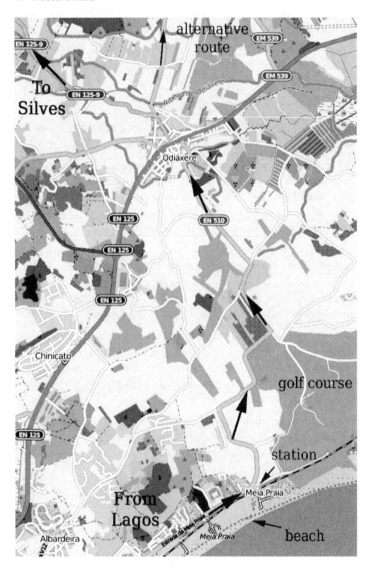

14. Odiaxere

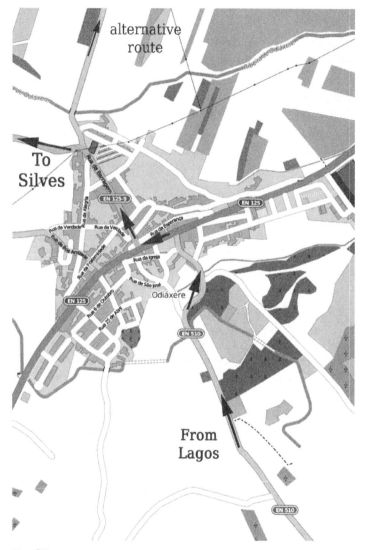

For **Silves**, see Map 1 on page 37.

LOULÉ CONNECTION

Overview

This section provides two extra days of riding, linking Silves – at the start/finish of the main **Touring Circuit** – with Loulé.

Going **east** from Silves, the route takes you inland through farmland, small villages and hill country that sees a tiny fraction of the huge number of visitors on the coast.

Coming back **west** from Loulé, you'll experience the other side of the Algarve: seeing some of its gorgeous beaches and a few of the resort towns where most tourists spend almost the entirety of their holidays.

Be warned, though, that the coastal route is only advised out of season when roads through this area are relatively quiet – attempt it at a busy time and you may have to cope with very heavy levels of tourist traffic, some of it on quite narrow roads.

One big advantage of getting to (or starting from) Loulé is that it's only a short distance from Faro and its airport.

You *can* ride there from Faro but the immediate surroundings of the Algarve's main city are not wonderful for cycling. If you do want to ride, it's just over 21km to Loulé taking a relatively traffic-free route (see information on **transport links** on page 106), or about 16 minutes on the train (which carries bikes) and then a straightforward 6km ride.

The other plus point is that Loulé provides an alternative start point for heading north into the Alentejo – for more details see the **Almodôvar Loop** (page 128).

Distance & difficulty

The routes suggested involve a 61.1km ride going east from Silves and a 71.7km ride going west from Loulé.

There are no major hills on either route, although the inland route does involve more climbing.

The only potential hazard on the coastal route is heavy traffic if attempting to ride this route during the holiday season (May to September).

Shorter versions

There are options to shorten both days, reducing the route east from Silves to 53km and the way west to a minimum of 55km. (For details see the **directions** for each day below.)

DAY ONE: SILVES – LOULÉ

Overview

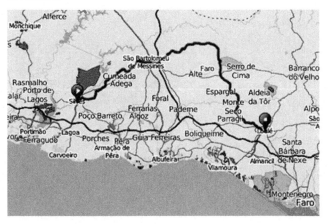

The ride starts from the same point as the **Touring Circuit** – on the N124 at the bottom of the old town, opposite the old bridge over the Rio Arade.

Leaving town, the route follows some minor roads by the river then uses a combination of the N124 (which is not overly busy) and a smaller road running parallel, taking you north-east towards the large village of São Bartolomeu de Messines.

The terrain gradually rises towards Messines and there's one serious climb on the road parallel with the N124, which is also the steepest section of the day.

There's a slight descent into Messines. Beyond the village the road climbs steadily but mostly quite gently as the route continues north-east into a very quiet rural area of fields and rolling hills.

At just over halfway, the route turns south. The road gets more undulating, with some bigs ups and downs as you then head through Benafim Grande and across the Ribeira de Algibre.

There's one last climb south of the river and then it's generally downhill along some country roads before the final run into Loulé.

Stats

Distance: 61.1km
Total elevation gain: +927m/-752
Maximum incline: 12.9%

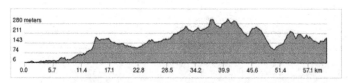

To download a map with full ride profiles, available as .gpx file etc., see: ridewithgps.com/routes/7573053

Alternative routes

The simplest option if you want to shorten the ride and reduce the amount of climbing would be to just follow the N124 from Silves to Benafim Grande and then continue on the main route.

This would reduce the distance to about 53km and the total climbing to 771m.

It's not a bad option – the N124 is relatively quiet and in good condition. The scenery is also quite attractive but nothing like as pretty or interesting as following the main route.

DIRECTIONS: SILVES – LOULÉ

1. **(1.5km)** Head north-east along the N124 with the river on your right and the castle up to your left.

   Go straight on at the junction with the N124-1 and follow the river and its line of palm trees around the south-east side of the town.

   Continue across the next roundabout and keep going until you see a mini-roundabout at a junction off to the right of the N124.

   Note: There are several **cafés** and a Lidl **supermarket** off to the left as you follow the river around town. (For more information on Silves see page 28.)

2. **(5.1km)** Turn right at the mini-roundabout – there's a blue *turismo rural* sign – on to the M1152.

   You're very quickly out of town and into an area of citrus orchards that continues until you reach a bridge over the Rio Arade.

   About 400m after crossing the river, you'll come to a left turn opposite a raised terrace on your right.

   Turn left here, continuing on the M1152 and running parallel with the Arade for about 2.3km.

   The road turns to follow the N124, which is raised above the M1152, before coming up to a T-junction.

3. **(2.4km)** Turn right on the N124 and follow it for 1.4km to the next left turn, signposted 'Barragem do Arade' (brown sign).

   Turn left on the M124-3 and follow it for 1km until you pass a **café/restaurant** on the left and come to a fork in the road.

4. **(6.2km)** Bear right on the M1116-1, signposted 'Gregórios' and 'Canhestros'. The road starts to climb from here but it's a steady, easy ascent on a very pleasant, single-track lane past fields, orchards and white-painted smallholdings.

   The surface deteriorates a bit as you head north-east and after about 4km the gradient begins to increase. The landscape also gets a bit wilder and more wooded.

   The steepest section (up to almost 13%) is where the road turns south and heads up and over a ridge of small hills.

A short way past the top of the climb, the road comes to a junction where you want to bear left towards the hamlet of Corte (no signpost).

Follow the road around several bends and through more small fields and scatted houses, heading north-east until you come down to a T-junction on the N124.

5. **(5.2km)** Turn left, signposted 'S. B. de Messines', and follow the N124. There isn't much of a shoulder but this road is rarely busy and is mostly fairly straight.

It's also generally flat or downhill towards the first turn-off for Messines (which would take you into a complicated one-way system).

Do not take this turning but stay on the N124, which goes up a small hill and then descends to a roundabout.

Turn left (third exit) on the N264, which takes you almost back on yourself as it heads roughly north into the middle of the village.

Note: Messines is pleasant enough but not that interesting. If you want to bypass the centre then take the first turning on the right, signposted 'Alte'. This takes you to the roundabout in **Point 6** below, where you again go right.

As you approach the historic centre, you pass an old cinema and a small municipal market building on the left.

On the right you'll see a branch of Banco Espirito Santo (green sign) at a junction signposted 'A2 Lisboa' and 'Alte'. There's also an Alisuper **supermarket** just before the bank.

The church and other older buildings lie straight ahead. However, because of the town's one-way system if you do go exploring it's easiest to come back to this junction.

6. **(1.6km)** Turn right towards Alte and take the second exit when you come to a roundabout on to Rua António Aleixo.

After 200m turn left at a small crossroads and then right at the next T-junction. You're now on a road that goes more or less due east out of town.

As you leave Messines, the road takes you under a bridge carrying the main 1C1 Faro-Lisbon road.

About 300m beyond the IC1 bridge the road curves slightly to the right and there's a junction on the left.

7. **(15.2km)** Go left, signposted 'Fonte João Luis'. The next 1km is on a flat, quiet road heading into an area of fields and scattered houses.

After passing under the A22 motorway, the road gets even quieter, climbing slightly as it continues north-east to the hamlet of Bica, where you'll see a sharper hill with several wind turbines on it to the right.

About 1km beyond Bica the road bends around to the right and you pass a **café** on the left. There's not much else around but small fields, wooded hills and the occasional farm or cluster of houses.

The road climbs again but the gradient is only very gentle, although the hills to either side get a bit closer and more rugged.

The road becomes the M542, taking you east past several hamlets and through an extremely pretty and unspoilt area of countryside.

Eventually, you will come to a junction where the M542 curves to the left (signposted 'Sobradinho', 'Cortinhola' and 'Almdôdovar') and another, unsignposted road goes off to the right.

8. **(5.9km)** Turn right and head south. There's a steep climb from this junction going up over some wooded hills.

The incline reaches over 12% but it's a good road and only about 600m before you're back on the flat and then going downhill again.

The road turns into the M1089 – this comes in from your right but you have right of way and just keep going south.

Note: As you approach Benafim Grande, the hills to your left include a protected area of limestone cliffs known as the **Rocha da Pena**.

There are walks here as well as opportunities to spot the local flora and fauna, including lots of birds. (For more information see page 162.)

There's another steady but gentle climb as you skirt the edge of the Rocha da Pena area, followed by a downhill and one more very minor hill.

The M1089 continues south to a roundabout on the N124 just outside the village of Benafim Grande – there's a small **café** off to the left.

9. **(6.7km)** Go across the roundabout and N124, and then continue straight on again in 200m to join the M524-2.

The road heads south-east, going down the side of the valley at a 45° angle. (At this point the route overlaps with the shorter version of the *Alte and the Caldeirão Foothills* day ride).

After just over 2km of lovely steady downhill the M524-2 reaches the bottom of the valley and starts to climb again. The incline reaches 9.9% on this section but there's a good surface and most of the hill is a lot more gentle.

It's less than 1km to the top of the hill. After that, the road runs more or less flat for about 500m before a last gentle climb to the village of Alto Fica.

From this point the road becomes the M524, and it's downhill again all the way to a junction with the M524-1.

10. **(2.4km)** Go straight on here – there's a sign for the Ribeira de Algibre, with a small **café** on the right just beyond.

After crossing the river, the road starts to climb. However, the gradient is very gentle as you head up the south side of the valley and into the hills.

You'll come to a small group of houses with a road on the right, going to Monte Ruivo and another turning on the left.

11. **(4.8km)** Go left on an unmarked single-track lane. The climb gets steeper here – reaching over 9% in a couple of places – but going this way saves you 2km of riding and slightly less climbing overall.

After climbing a hillside covered with scrubby trees, the ride levels out and comes into an area of small fields, before reaching a T-junction (unmarked) on the M1177.

Turn left – from here it's an undulating ride through quiet countryside and small settlements almost all of the rest of the way to Loulé.

In about 600m you meet a road coming in almost parallel on your right and then reach another junction.

Turn left, signposted 'Sobradinho' and 'Alfeição'. The road curves to the right and in about 700m comes up to a kind of crossroads where the road straight ahead is closed to cars with a barrier.

Turn right and follow the lane on a gentle (mostly) downhill for the next 1.4km until you come to a left turn.

Go left and uphill for 300m, which will bring you to the next junction with a much better surfaced, two-lane road going off to the right.

12. **(3.3km)** Turn right on to the new road, which in about 1.7km will take you to a roundabout almost on the edge of Loulé.

Take the third exit (N270) towards the city centre. After about 1.2km there is another roundabout where you go right (first exit) to follow the one-way system towards the *centro*.

Note: Although this route is not the most direct, going straight ahead involves a lot of narrow, cobbled streets so this is the best option for cyclists.

The N270 becomes the M1305 – taking you past a large Modelo/Continente **supermarket** on the right – and continues straight on at another roundabout as it skirts the old town.

The next roundabout is marked with statues of two cyclists, one triumphant, one exhausted.

Note: There's a **bike shop** next to the roundabout – S Bikes. I've never been in there and there's no company website (only a basic Facebook page) so I can't tell you any more about them.

13. **(800m)** Take the second exit on to Rua Eng. Duarte Pacheco, which runs east past the GNR station and a section of the remaining city walls.

The street gets narrower and more residential from here, taking you past brown signs for the *centro histórico*.

Keep going straight on for another few blocks and you will come to a set of traffic lights with the *centro* signposted to the left.

Turn left here on to Avenida Marçal Pacheco, which in about 200m will bring you to a large roundabout which marks the end of the route.

OVERNIGHT: LOULÉ

Loulé (pop 23,100) is the biggest inland town in the Algarve, lying roughly 18km to the north–west of Faro. Mostly a quite modern, fairly high-rise place, it does also have an interesting network of old cobbled streets just to the south-west of the centre.

The city is best known these days for its enormous, open-air Saturday markets, selling pretty much anything and everything, although it also has a decent daily (except Sunday) produce market.

Loulé is known across the Algarve for its Easter carnival, a three-day Brazilian-style event which is one of the biggest in the country.

A popular summer event is Noite Branca (*White Night*) when locals and visitors come together for a festival where people – all wearing white – wander the streets dressed as fantasy figures, to a backdrop of live music and dance.

Loulé's origins probably date back to Roman times, although there are prehistoric remains in the area dating back to 4000BC. By the time the Moors invaded in the early 8th century, Loulé was already an important town in the region.

The city's market and castle were both established in the 13th century after the Christian reconquest. There's not much left of the castle now – three towers and some connecting walls – but the remains now house Loulé's municipal archaeological museum.

In 2013, archaeologists also completed an excavation of a baths complex dating back to the Moorish period.

Most of the sights of interest to visitors lie in a compact area around the main church – although if you're really bored (or uncertain what to do with your spare garden produce) there's always the Museológico de Frutos Secos (*Museum of Dried Fruit*).

As you'd expect in a large town, there's also a good range of shops and restaurants, plus cinemas, a sports centre, swimming pools etc.

Economically, Loulé is one of the most prosperous towns in the 'Golden Triangle' at the centre of the Algarve, and the city's population has grown fairly steadily in recent decades.

Supermarkets

There are plenty of options in Loulé, including a large **Modelo/Continente** store off the M1305 as you come around the south-west side of the city centre.

Other options include two **Pingo Doce** stores: a small shop on Rua David Teixeira to the north-east of the centre, and a much larger outlet just off to the right of the N396 heading south out of town.

Just beyond the second Pingo, on the other side of the N396 there's also a large **Lidl**.

Bike shops

There are two bike shops close to the centre of the city:

S Bikes on Avenida Andrade de Sousa (roundabout at junction of N396 and M1305). *Tel:* 289 463 219

Freebike in Rua Dr Francisco Sá Carneiro (south-east of the centre between the N270 and N125-4).
Tel: 289 412 314 *Web:* freebike.pt.vu/

Transport links

Train:

If starting your ride from Loulé (or ending it there), the easiest way to get to and from Faro is probably by train.

Comboios de Portugal (CP) runs nine (regional) trains a day from Faro to Loulé. The journey takes around 16mins and tickets currently cost €1.90.

Loulé train station is 6km south-west of the city. It's not the most pleasant road in places but perfectly rideable: see **Points 1-3** of the Loulé-Silves route below – and follow in reverse.

For more information on the region's rail service and getting to the station at Faro from the airport, see the notes on trains in the Silves transport links section (see page 29).

Bicycle:

If you want to ride from Faro, many roads around the city and its airport are extremely busy.

I've never tried riding out of Faro myself, but one possible route (starting from outside the cathedral) would be as follows:

- **(1.2km)** Head north for 250m and then right on to Av. Dr Julio F. De Almeida Carrapato, which takes you to the N125.
- **(6km)** Turn right on the N125 for about 100m and then take the first left on the M518, signposted 'Patacão' and 'Conceição'. Follow the road north and then to the west, crossing over the N2 at a set of traffic lights and continuing west (follow signs for Patacão and the A22) towards the N125/IC4.
- **(5.8km)** Just before the main road, turn right, signposted 'Portimão' and 'S.ta. B. Nexe'. Head north on the M520 towards Santa Barbara de Nexe, turning left just before the village, signposted 'Almancil' and 'Esteval'.
- **(7.9km)** Turn right at the next roundabout, signposted 'Loulé. Go north for 400m and left at the next roundabout. The M520-1, takes you west before joining the N124-1 for the last 6km.

Accommodation

Camping:

There is no campsite anywhere in the immediate area – the nearest is on the coast at Quarteira.

Hotels & Guest Houses:

Loulé Jardim Hotel (3), Praça Manuel de Arriaga, 8100-665 Loulé.
Tel: 289 413 094/5 *Email:* hotel@loulejardimhotel.com
Web: loulejardimhotel.com

Hospedaria Dom Fernando, Travessa do Mercado, 8100-648 Loulé.
Tel: 289 415 553 *Email:* h.domfernando@netcabo.pt

Loulé Coreto Hostel, Avenida José da Costa Mealha, 8100-500 Loulé.
Tel: 289 411 063 *Email:* loulecoretohostel@gmail.com
Web: loulecoretohostel.com

For more options, including accommodation across the region surrounding Loulé, see:
cm-loule.pt/pt/menu/147/alojamento.aspx

DAY TWO: LOULÉ – SILVES

Overview

This route from Loulé to Silves takes you in a big loop to the south-west, passing through several of the Algarve's biggest holiday resorts – and visiting some of its most popular beaches.

Going this way is probably not a good idea anytime between May and September when visitor numbers along the coast mean many of the roads in this area can get horrendously busy.

However, if you're cycling through out of season and want to see what it is that draws those hordes of sun worshippers then this is your chance.

None of the cycling is difficult. It's mostly downhill from Loulé to the coast and apart from a few minor ups and downs you're unlikely to need your low gears anywhere along the way.

This isn't all pretty riding. The resort areas can feel like an endless procession of tower blocks, hotel developments, holiday villas and golf courses.

On the other hand, this is the 'real' Algarve in the sense that this coastal strip is what drives the region's economy – and you do get to ride along the prom right next to some gorgeous beaches.

There are also some more rural stretches and the area west of Armação de Pêra, before you turn inland, is extremely pretty. Once you've turned north and crossed the N125 towards Silves, the riding is also nearly all very rural, taking you past citrus groves and fields towards the Algarve's ancient capital.

Stats

Distance: 71.7km
Total elevation gain: +625m/-799
Maximum incline: 9.5%

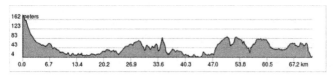

To download a map with full ride profiles, available as .gpx file etc., see: ridewithgps.com/routes/7809523

Alternative (shorter) routes

There are two options (details follow main route) for cutting the overall distance.

The first, which takes 6.1km off the total, bypasses the resorts of Quarteira and Vilamoura by turning west not long after Loulé then turning south-west towards Albufeira and rejoining the main route.

The second cuts out the final beach visit at Benagil (which has a very pretty cove set in rugged cliffs) and cuts off 9.9km.

Extension/side trip

West of Albufeira there's an opportunity to detour off the main route and visit the beaches at Galé and Salgados, both part of a long, long stretch of golden sand to the south-west of the resort of Armação de Pêra.

The main route along the M526 isn't particularly inspiring so this side trip offers a much more scenic option –plus the chance to paddle/swim at a couple of stunning beaches that are a lot wilder and not as busy as those at the resort towns.

The side trip only adds 4.7km to the total distance – although it does involve crossing a lagoon on a boardwalk and a short section of dirt track.

DIRECTIONS: LOULÉ – SILVES

1. **(800m)** Head south along Avenida Marçal Pacheco from the roundabout in the centre of town at the junction with the N270.

   After just over 200m turn right at the traffic lights at the junction with Rua Eng. Duarte Pacheco – there are local signposts to the *'Cemitério'*, *'Bombeiros'* and 'GNR'.

   Follow the road for around 500m, riding past the old city walls (on the right) until you come to a roundabout at the junction between the N396 and the M1305.

   Note: This section retraces the route used coming in to Loulé from Silves.

2. **(800m)** Turn left (third exit) on a dual carriageway section of the N396, which takes you past the Pingo Doce and Lidl **supermarkets**.

   This road can be busy at times but not always and has a smooth new surface – plus it's pretty much downhill all the way from Loulé to the coast.

   Go straight on at the first roundabout and stay on the dual carriageway for around another 400m. Just beyond a bus stop the new road starts to curve around to the left and there is a slip road going off to the right (straight ahead).

3. **(4.7km)** Turn right, signposted *'Zona Industrial'*. There is also a village sign at the start of the slip road for Campina de Baixo.

   The slip road will bring you down to another roundabout on the old N396, where you want to go straight on (second exit), also signposted 'Franqueda'.

   The next few kilometres include some new sections around various industrial parks and roundabouts, plus older and rougher stretches as the scenery becomes more rural.

   The N396 can be busy at times and is also fairly narrow in places, particularly after you've gone under the A22 motorway so some caution is advised on this road. There are also several bends as you approach the village of Franqueada and the turning for Loulé's railway station (to the right).

About 800m after crossing the railway line you come to a roundabout on the main east-west N125 road.

4. **(4.4km)** Turn left (third exit) on to the N125 – signposted 'Loulé', 'A22', and 'Faro/Almancil'.

Warning: the N125 is the main east-west road across the Algarve and can be very busy. However, you're only on it for less than 1km and there is a shoulder, although you'll have to watch for traffic coming from various side roads and entrances.

> After 900m, just ahead of a large sign for a roundabout, is a right turn, with a small sign for 'Pereiras'.

> Turn right here and then – after about 150m – go left at a kind of T-junction.

> This takes you on a smooth bit of road under the new N396 main road to the resort of Quarteira.

> After going through an underpass the road parallels the N396 for a short distance and then heads off into a much quieter area.

The road heads roughly south-south-west, gently dropping in height, passing some fields and areas of woodland but also quite a few houses and villas in private grounds. Some of the villas look fairly traditional, others are much more fancy-looking. (Watch out for the Quinta do Galvão on your left which looks as if it's escaped from some Arabian Nights fantasy.)

Just after passing a small industrial estate on the left you come to a T-junction on a larger road.

5. **(2.4km)** Turn right – signposted 'Quarteira' – on to the M527-2, which will take you all the way into the centre of the resort and out the other side.

The first 1km or so on the gently undulating M527-2 is a bit scruffy in places, with a mixture of unkempt fields, scattered houses and occasional derelict building.

Coming into Quarteira, the road widens into a dual carriageway with a line of trees down the middle strip. You pass an increasing number of apartment blocks on either side.

As the road comes into the resort it curves to the right and you'll see glimpses of the sea between the buildings. Keep going to the first roundabout.

Note: This is your first opportunity to visit the beach. If you turn left at the roundabout it's a short ride to the seafront. Go straight across at the first junction on to a pedestrianised street and the promenade is at the other end.

If you want, you can follow the prom all the way along, riding right next to a gorgeous sandy beach. The wide pedestrianised strip runs out next to the Restaurante Rosa Branca.

Beyond here you need to join the road – going past an Alisuper **supermarket** on the right. Stay parallel with the beach (passing the blue and white market building). The road doglegs, right and left, around a busy parking area but turn to the right again and it will take you back to the main route out of town to the west.

6. **(2.1km)** If you're not going to the beach, continue straight on along the M527-2/Avenida Sá Carneiro.

The road through town is a wide, tree-lined avenue with service roads running parallel and hotels and tower blocks to either side.

Keep going through several roundabouts and follow the main avenue as it curves to the north-west and turns inland. By the sixth roundabout the road turns almost north.

After one more roundabout you should see a set of signposts with a blue sign for 'Vilamoura' to the left and 'Loulé' and *'outros destinos'* (other destinations) to the right. Just beyond here the road splits and you want to take the left lane, as you approach a set of traffic lights at the top of Av. Dr Carlos Mota Pinto.

7. **(3.9km)** Turn left towards Vilamoura on the Estrada de Quarteira, which will take you north-west out of town past more hotels, apartments, golf courses, and lots of palm and pine trees. (This side of town is a lot greener and a bit more low-rise.)

Keep going past several junctions and roundabouts, following signs for Vilamoura 'centro'. The road turns north for a bit and you then need to fork north-west, again following 'centro' signs along a wide, manicured boulevard lined with palms and lots of subtropical shrubs and trees.

Leaving town the road becomes single-carriageway and quite a lot narrower, turning north again. A short distance before a roundabout (the first in a while) you'll see signs for the 'EN125' ahead and 'Estrada de Albufeira' to the left.

Note: If the road's busy and you want to get out of the traffic there are cycle/footpaths, including boardwalk sections, along much of the road around Vilamoura.

8. **(4.8km)** Turn left on to the Estrada de Albufeira, a two-lane road that takes you roughly west-north-west for about 3km, climbing very slightly as it heads inland past expanses of pines and various holiday complexes.

At the sixth roundabout, turn right (first exit) and head north for just under 500m to another roundabout, next to a BP petrol station, at a junction with the M526.

Turn left. This road can be a bit busy, particularly during the holiday season but does have a narrow shoulder. The scenery also gets a bit more rural as you head away from Vilamoura.

The M526 takes you south-west across the small Ribeira de Quarteira. As you cross the bridge over the river, you will see a large sign for the *'Concelho Albufeira'* (Albufeira County) and a smaller one for the 'Freguesia de Olhos de Água' (which translates as something like the parish of the Eyes of the Water).

9. **(16.7km)** From the bridge over the Quarteira river keep going along the M526 – this road changes name a couple of times along the way but will take you all the way through Albufeira and almost to the village of Pêra.

Much of this section is not that interesting with a seemingly endless parade of holiday villas and tourist complexes. However, there are opportunities to detour to some stunning beaches – see **Galé and Salgados** notes on page 120.

East of Albufeira the landscape is semi-rural and

fairly pretty, but with clusters of villas dotted everywhere and a fairly suburban feel in places.

Then, about 6km from the Quarteira river, the road turns into a dual carriageway with palm trees down the middle (and another cycle path off to the left). Shortly after, the massed apartment blocks begin as you come into Albufeira.

The M562 is the Avenida dos Descobrimentos as it goes through Albufeira and there are a few short but sharp ups and downs that might come as a bit of a shock after the very easy riding until this point.

Note: These directions take you straight through Albufeira and you won't see much of interest along the way.

It's only a short detour to the old town at the centre of the resort, which is quite pretty. The town also has a beautiful beach (assuming you can see it for the bodies) and it's obvious why Albufeira became such a popular tourist destination.

On the downside, the old town is the usual maze of little streets, many of them pedestrianised and cobbled, and finding your way can be tricky. Albufeira is also unlikely to be a cultural highpoint of any visit to Portugal.

If you do want to see the centre, the easiest thing is probably to turn left when you get to a roundabout with a bizarre sculpture of two large worms, one green and one red. Go south on Rua de Dunfermline and then right at the next roundabout onto Avenida Infante Dom Henrique, which will take you right down to the clifftops just east of the old town.

To escape, just head north and find your way back to the Avenida dos Descobrimentos.

It takes about 6km and lots of roundabouts to get clear of Albufeira's centre, after which the M526 reverts to a normal two-lane road. The area heading west towards Vale de Parra includes some fields and trees but also a lot of strung-out villages and small developments.

The M526 comes to a roundabout in Vale de Parra with signposts for 'Pêra' straight ahead.

10. **(2.8km)** Unless you're turning left for the beach at Galé (see page 120) keep

going straight on along the M526.

Beyond Vale de Parra, the landscape gradually starts to feel a bit more open and rural, and not so heavily developed. The riding along this stretch is also all fast and easy – on a very gently undulating road.

About 2km beyond the roundabout in Vale de Parra, the M526 crosses a small bridge and you leave the *concelho* of Albufeira and cross into the Silves area and the *freguesia* of Pêra.

From here the M526 continues north-west for just under 2km then comes up a small incline to another roundabout with Pêra signposted right and Armação de Pêra ahead.

11. **(1.4km)** Take the second exit – there are no signposts on the roundabout itself.

In just under 1km, you come to another roundabout, where you again take the second exit.

The road then runs almost dead flat for 400m across some open fields, crossing a trickle of a stream that is the Ribeira de Alcantarilha.

12. **(1.1km)** Just metres before a welcome sign for the Alcantarilha district, turn left onto an unmarked, single-track lane and continue south for 500m.

At the next junction turn right and follow another tiny lane which will take you south-west for about 600m to join the N269-1 on the outskirts of Armação de Pêra just before a roundabout.

13. **(1.8km)** Turn left on to the N269-1 (there's a pedestrian crossing if the road's busy). On the other side of the roundabout, the N269-1 turns into a wide dual carriageway that will take you straight through the resort.

At the sixth roundabout the road becomes the M530-1 and starts to turn inland.

Note: In many ways, Armação de Pêra is like a smaller version of Albufeira with masses of apartment blocks and more modern development packed in above a gorgeous beach.

If you want to see the town and its beach, the simplest option is to turn left at the fourth roundabout on the N269-1 – signposted 'praia' and 'centro'.

If you keep going straight ahead from the roundabout (which involves going the wrong way down a cobbled one-way street at the end) you will reach the Avenida Beira Mar, a pedestrianised street that follows the seafront.

Go left and it will take you down to the beach, tourist office, and narrow streets of this one time fishing village's original centre.

Turn right and it will bring you on to a road that runs above some low cliffs and past the back of the Holiday Inn Algarve before joining the M530-1 as it leaves town.

14. **(5km)** The M530-1 climbs a little as it leaves Armação and heads around the back of another resort called Alporchinos.

    After heading towards Porches for 3.1km, you should see a left turn, signposted 'Lagoa' and 'Carvoeiro'. Turn left here – and then in about 350m turn left again.

    It's all much more rural and scenic now as you head west on a quiet country road. Turn left at the first T-junction, signposted 'Lagoa/EN125'.

Head west for about 400m to another T-junction, on the M1154.

15. **(4.1km)** Turn left here to follow the main route (or go right if you're following the alternative option detailed below).

The road runs south over sandy heathland towards a roundabout where you turn right (first exit), signposted 'Benagil', still on the M1154.

After just under 1km, the road curves left, with a brown signpost for the beach at Benagil. It's downhill from here through some of the prettiest countryside of the day.

The road descends sharply towards a small car park above a sandy cove wedged into an opening in the cliffs.

Note: Praia de Benagil offers the last chance to get some sand between your toes before turning inland for Silves.

It's also a very different scene from the long sweeping stretches of sand further east.

The beach isn't much more than 100m wide and is framed by a backdrop of rocky cliffs. There are paths along the cliffs to either side and more small coves tucked into the jagged coastline.

You can also take boat trips from Benagil to visit some dramatic sea caves hidden inside the local cliffs.

16. **(6.7km)** Continue up the hill on the other side of the narrow valley for 300m, which will bring you to a small roundabout.

Turn right, signposted 'Lagoa'. You are now on the M1273, a pleasant, fairly rural road heading roughly north-east and climbing at a steady pace. (The road climbs about 60m over a distance of 1.8km from the beach, with the steepest section coming straight after leaving the cove.)

After 2km the M1273 comes to a roundabout. Turn right here, signposted 'Porches' and 'Caramujeira'.

In another 1.1km you come to the next roundabout. Go left here (third exit), signposted 'Lagoa', 'Portimão' and 'Silves' (brown sign).

From here, it's 3.1km along an undulating road past scrubby fields and scattered houses, initially heading almost due north and then

swinging to the north-west as you approach Lagoa.

Go straight on at the first roundabout on the edge of town, which will bring you up to a set of traffic lights at a junction on the main N125.

17. **(6.8km)** Turn left on the N125 and then immediately go right, signposted 'Silves' and 'centro'.

In just over 100m you come to a small roundabout behind a Netto **supermarket**.

Turn right here (first exit) into Rua Francisco Sá Carneiro and keep going until you reach a 'stop' sign.

Turn right, signposted 'Lameiras' (ignore the sign for Silves going straight ahead as this takes you on to a very busy route).

After about 1km there's a fork in the road. Go left, signposted 'Silves', on to a narrow lane past fields and orchards.

In about 900m you will come to a small crossroads where you turn left and head north on Rua de Lobito, which takes you over the A22 motorway and past areas of horticultural polytunnels.

Shortly after the motorway, the road twists right and then left before coming out into more open countryside and continuing north. It becomes the M1154 as it heads towards the small settlement around Silves train station and comes to a T-junction just to the south of a level crossing.

18. **(1.9km)** Turn right, go across the level crossing and up the (small) hill ahead. Go straight on at the roundabout and down the other side of the hill – you'll see Silves straight ahead as you start to descend.

Follow the road to the right as you come down on to the N124-1. There's a wide shoulder at the junction. This is replaced by a pavement as you come down the hill but it's a straight road with good visibility and should be safe.

Keep going down and take the left-turn lane at the junction for Silves – also signposted 'Lisboa'.

Go across the Rio Arade on the N124-1 and then turn left on the N124 until you reach the steps opposite the old bridge, which mark the end of the ride.

The centre of the old town, including the cathedral and castle ruins, are off to your right here.

For information on Silves, including accommodation, see page 28.

Note: As you come down the hill you'll see a turning to the left leading to an old arched bridge. You can go this way, which is quite pretty, but the bridge is pedestrian-only and there are steps down on the other side.

Alternative routes

There are a couple of options for reducing the distance of this stage:

You can completely avoid the resorts of Quarteira and Vilamoura, and cut 6.1km from the total distance by turning west before reaching the N125.

To do this, begin by turning right in Franqueda – see **Point 3** (page 110) – and following signs for the *'Estação'* (train station).

- Continue past the station and along a quiet country lane towards Vale de Judeu. Turn right at the first T-junction on the M1295 and then left at the next T-junction.

- The road wiggles around a bit, going west then south. Just before you cross the railway line turn right on a tiny, unmarked lane through fruit orchards.

- The lane turns right and in 600m comes to a tiny crossroads, where you go left and uphill into Caminho da Soalheira (look for a small sign on the wall).

- After 1.1km, go across a staggered crossroads (left and right) on the M1293. Continue west along this lane past lots of houses to a T-junction on the M1294.

- Turn left and in about 200m you come to the N125. You do have to turn right on the main road here but you're only on the N125 for 450m and it's dead straight with good visibility.

- Turn left on the M526, signposted to 'Albufeira' (blue sign), 'praias' (brown sign) and 'Olhos de Água'. The M526 then rejoins the main route towards the end of **Point 8**.

You can also cut 9.9km from the total by missing out the cove at Benagil – although this also means missing some of the day's prettiest scenery.

To do this, simply turn right when you reach the M1154 – see **Point 14**. Keep heading north to a set of traffic lights on the N125, where you go straight across – signposted 'Urzais'.

Continue north and this road will become the Rua de Lobito and rejoin the main route – see **Point 16** (page 117).

Gale and Salgados

Most of the landscape between Quarteira and Armação de Pêra is fairly unremarkable and overdeveloped. However, if you like golden beaches then the coast itself offers some simply gorgeous spots.

This side trip visits two of the best beaches on this stretch of the Algarve. Neither will be empty at peak season but they are also nothing like as developed as the main resorts and feel a lot wilder.

The side trip itself is about 7.5km and replaces a 2.8km section on the M526 – so effectively adds 4.7km to the day's overall distance.

It also involves using some sections of boardwalk and dirt track, although this should be perfectly rideable if dry.

To get to the beaches, turn left at the roundabout in Vale de Parra – see **Point 10** above.

- Follow the brown beach signs for Galé, which will take you straight on at the first roundabout and right at the second. This will bring you to a small car park right next to a stunning sandy beach.
- From the far end of the car park at Galé, go back and then turn left on a dirt path that runs parallel with the top of the beach.
- Follow this around the back of a white beach restaurant and then turn right, going directly away from the beach.
- The dirt track will turn into a sealed road leading up past some villas and bring you to a T-junction, where you turn left on Estrada dos Salgados.

Note: If you don't want to take the track, ride back to the second roundabout from the car park at Galé, turn left and then take the next left into Estrada dos Salgados.

- Turn right at the end of Est. dos Salgados and then left (second exit) at the next roundabout – brown signpost for 'Salgados' beach.

- Keep going through the next three roundabouts and the road will end at a car park next to where the Lagoa dos Saldagos (*Salgados lagoon*) meets another huge expanse of golden beach.

- There's a footbridge across the lagoon and a wooden boardwalk runs around the back of the dunes and along the edge of the water, ending at another car park on the opposite side of the lagoon.

- Head inland on a dirt track away from the beach. In about 700m the surface becomes sealed.

- Follow the lane back across fields until it curves to the right and comes to a roundabout where the M526 goes to Pêra, and you turn left (fourth exit) and resume the main route from **Point 11** above.

MAPS: LOULÉ CONNECTION

15. São Bartolomeu de Messines

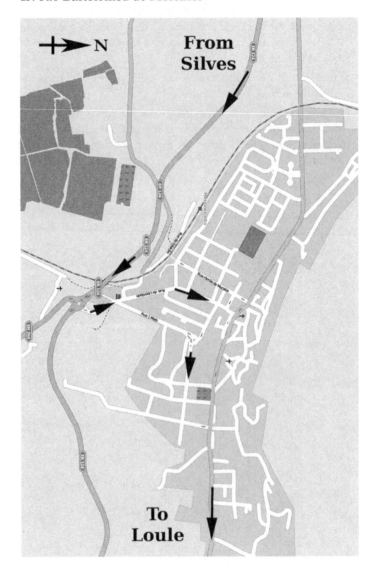

16. Loulé

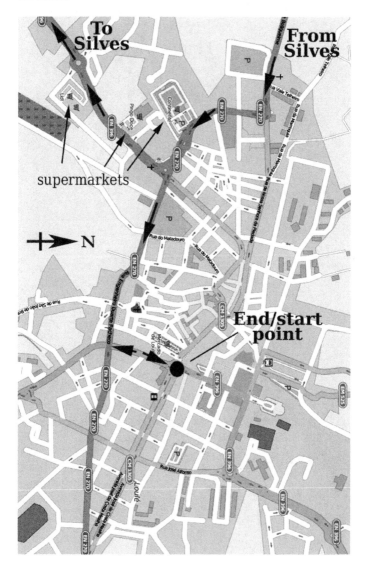

17. Loulé station

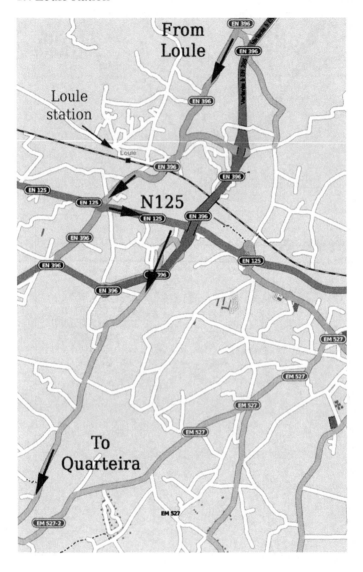

18. Quarteira & Vilamoura

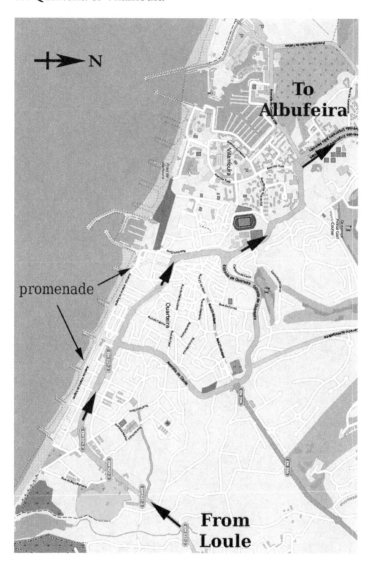

19. Albufeira

20. Armação de Pêra

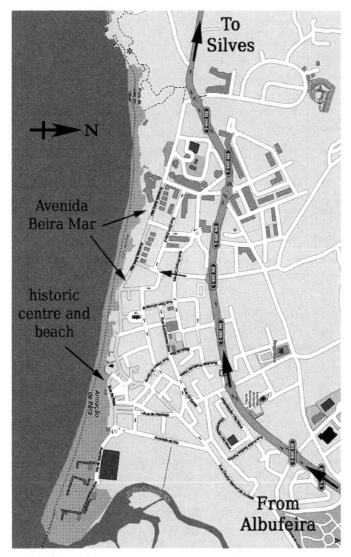

For **Silves**, see Map 1 on page 37.

ALMODÔVAR LOOP

Overview

This section provides a north-south loop connecting Loulé in the central Algarve with Almodôvar in the southern Alentejo.

It's spectacular scenery: much of it quite remote and wild, with few settlements of any kind along the way, particularly on the way south. There's also some serious climbing to do – see **distance & difficulty** below.

The loop not only provides two days of very scenic riding that could be used to extend the main **Touring Circuit** but could also be useful for touring cyclists wanting to connect the Algarve and the Alentejo as part of a longer expedition – including linking with Pedal Portugal's *Alentejo Circuit* (see page 203).

Distance & difficulty

I've detailed the loop as a two-day trip: a 67.4km ride north mainly following the N2 and a 61.3km return journey over Malhão, one of the high points of the Serra de Caldeirão.

Fitter riders (not fully laden tourers) might want to contemplate doing this as a one-day, 129km challenge. But, be warned, neither day is an easy option.

The ride north, although beautiful, involves nearly 1,200m of ascent, including one section with about 7km of steady climbing (going up around 300m).

Coming south, the climbs are not as long or as high but the ride still involves almost 1,000m of ascent.

Unless you are seriously into hill-climbing, I would also definitely **not** recommend doing the loop the other way around if you are travelling with any luggage at all.

The ascent to Malhão from the south is used in February's *Volta ao Algarve*, used by many of the world's top professional cyclists as a warm-up for the season's big races.

The riders who take part in the Volta climb Malhão twice as part of a 164.5km stage (won in 2015 by Richie Porte, with Geraint Thomas taking the title for the overall event).

But before you contemplate replicating their efforts, be aware that the ascent from the south reaches an incline of over 19% (or 1:5 in old money).

Shorter versions

There are options to slightly shorten both days, which would also reduce the total amount of climbing. (For details see the **directions** for each day below.)

Going north, a more direct route from Loulé to join the N2 would reduce the distance by about 4.5km and cut out about 250m of climbing.

Coming south, taking a more direct route from Almodôvar towards Malhão would take 5km off the distance but only reduce the climbing by about 30m.

Together, this would give a there-and-back distance of just under 120km and a total ascent of 1,993m.

DAY ONE: LOULÉ – ALMODÔVAR

Overview

The ride starts from the centre of Loulé (which is about 6km north of the town's train station).

There's some gentle climbing to do leaving Loulé but you're soon out of town and riding in pleasant countryside on a good road.

After about 5km the route becomes more undulating, with some sharp ups and downs but nothing very long. (One of the worst climbs could also be missed out by bypassing the village of Querença.)

The scenery also gets a lot wilder, with the road twisting its way through some very pretty forested hills.

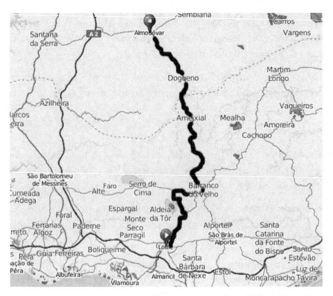

After about 16km of wriggling north, the route turns east on the N124. Following a short flattish section the day's big climb begins. It's about 7km of steady ascent to join the N2 and turn north again.

From here there's a bit more climbing to do but the route becomes much more rolling for the next 12km or so. After that you've got a huge descent for almost 14km – almost all of which is downhill.

The Ribeira do Vascão at the bottom of the hill marks the border between the Algarve and the Alentejo. From here you've got a couple more hills but nothing too major.

Approaching Almodôvar the terrain starts to really open out into the kind of low hills and open plains that are much more typical of the Alentejo.

Traffic should not be a problem unless there happens to be logging going on somewhere along the way. Otherwise, because the N2 is such a winding route, it doesn't attract a lot of vehicles; it's not a road to take if you're trying to get anywhere fast.

There are a few small villages with cafés on the N2, the largest is Ameixial about 45km into the ride.

However, there's not a lot else along the way and no particular sights to see other than miles and miles of forested hills and the occasional area of farmland.

Stats

Distance: 67.4km
Total elevation gain: +1166m/-1059
Maximum incline: 11.6%

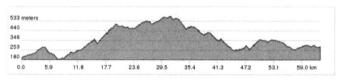

To download a map with full ride profile, available as .gpx file etc., see: ridewithgps.com/routes/7554755

Alternative routes

There's no way to avoid climbing if you want to go between the Algarve and the Alentejo. However, you can reduce the total ascent.

One option that would cut around 4.5km from the distance and about 250m of climbing is to simply stick on the N396 from Loulé instead of turning off near Querença.

The N396 joins the N124 further east than if you take the main route. If following the N396, simply turn right when you reach the N124 and join the N2 as described below.

If sticking to the main route you can also avoid a bit of a climb (just over 30m) by taking the M524 around Querença rather than going up into the village. However, this would be a bit of a shame as the village centre is definitely worth a look.

DIRECTIONS: LOULÉ – ALMODÔVAR

1. **(1.4km)** The ride starts from the large roundabout in the centre of town where the N270 meets the N125-4 (Avenida Marçal Pacheco) and the N396 (Avenida 25 de Abril).

   Go north for three blocks (about 250m) on the N396 to a set of traffic lights.

   You should see the entrance to the town's park about 50m ahead on the other side.

   Turn right here (still on the N396) and continue for just over 200m to a large roundabout with several palm trees in the centre.

   Take the third exit to follow the N396 along a wide, four-lane section with a narrow central reservation. The road climbs gently (1-3%) as it skirts the town.

   Go straight on at the next roundabout and you'll reach the edge of town by a third roundabout next to the town's sports centre – where there's a typically Portuguese lack of signposts!

2. **(7.5km)** Continue straight on (to the right of the sports centre) to keep following the N396.

   The road climbs steadily over the next 3km but with nowhere more than a 4.5% incline.

   There are houses to either side as you head roughly north-north-east away from Loulé but beyond them you can see wooded hills.

   It soon gets a lot more rural and you've then got around 3km of mostly downhill as you descend into the valley of the Ribeira das Mercés.

   The road rises again on the other side of the river but only gently as it takes you up to a left turn for Querença.

3. **(1.8km)** Turn left towards the village. It's a steady climb as you head north on the M524 but the views are marvellous!

Note: If you don't want to climb up into the village (saving about 30m of ascent), simply follow the M524 as it curves around the hill on which it sits and then turn right at the next crossroads, signposted 'Varzeas de Querença' and 'Corcitos'.

After about 400m you need to do a sharp left to go up

into the village centre. There's a kilometre of climbing from here, averaging about 5% but going up to 9%.

There's a lovely paved plaza around the church when you get to the top, surrounded by some immaculate white-painted houses – real 'picture postcard' Portugal. (There's also a **café** on the north side of the square for when you've had enough of looking at the scenery.)

The one-way system does a loop around the back of the church and then descends just as steeply on the other side, taking you down to a crossroads on the M524.

4. **(5.5km)** Go straight across the crossroads towards Varzeas de Querença and Corcitos.

You're on a narrow, single-track lane that continues down for about 750m, through an area of small fields/orchards, until it comes to a T-junction on the M510.

Turn right here (no signposts). The M510 runs more or less flat for a short distance and then starts to climb through the tiny settlement of Cerca Nova and up to the hamlet of Corcitos.

The road bends to the right in Corcitos and then the next descent begins. There's a bit of a bump in the middle, otherwise it drops around 80m over the next 2.7km.

After crossing a small bridge and passing the sign marking the edge of the Querença *freguesia* (parish), there's a gentle climb up to a T-junction on the N124.

5. **(7.5km)** Turn right on the N124, signposted 'Barranco do Velho'. You've got a couple of kilometres of gently undulating, mostly straight road from here.

After that, though, you've got about 6km of steady climbing, with an ascent of around 300m.

As the N124 enters an area of wooded hills, the road starts to twist and turn. However, none of the inclines are that severe – it's all below 10% and most is more like 5-8%.

Just over a third of the way up, you pass a right turn onto the N396 – but that's the only proper junction along the way until you come to the village of Barranco do Velho and reach the N2.

6. **(14.1km)** Turn left on the N2, signposted 'Lisboa', 'Beja' and 'Alcoutim'. The road continues to climb as it goes up through the village but it's only about 700m to the top of the hill (and an altitude of just over 500m).

There's not a lot to Barranco but there is a **café/ restaurant** on the right a few hundred metres after you join the N2.

By the time you get to the top of the hill you're back out into wild-looking hill country. The next 4km are undulating but generally downhill.

There's another **café** on the N2 in a hamlet called Cortelha but nothing in Vale Maria Dias another 1km further on.

Just beyond the second hamlet the road starts to go up again. It's not a continual climb; the road twists and dips as it winds its way through a landscape of wooded hills, occasional tiny settlements, areas of cork oak and grazing, and patches of wild scrubland.

In total the N2 climbs about 120m in height over the next 8km after Vale Maria Dias. After the crest of this hill the road continues to undulate but starts to drop in height.

As you come down a series of gentle curves, you'll see a white-painted house right next to the road with the letters 'J.A.E.' in tiles.

Note: This charming old house is a *Casa de Cantoneiros*, literally 'house of mending'. In the old days, this would be where the local road mender lived and it was his responsibility to keep his section of road in good condition, including tidying up the verges.

Many of these old houses are now derelict (and sadly often covered with graffiti). This one, however, apart from having its doors and windows blocked up, is in immaculate condition.

It also provides a stunning viewpoint looking out over the hills on the border of the Algarve and Alentejo regions – and makes an excellent picnic/rest stop before the final 30km to Almodôvar. (There's a shelter down in the trees on the north (downhill) side of the house.)

7. **(11.6km)** Keep going along the N2 from the Casa de Cantoneiros. The descent gets quite a lot steeper from here, with a couple of sweeping bends as you drop down towards the Alentejo plains.

There are a couple of short uphill sections but over the course of this section you are going to descend around 290m in height.

About halfway down the hill, the N2 passes through a larger village called Almexial, where you'll find a couple of basic **café/snack bars** but not much else.

At the bottom of the hill lies the Ribeira do Vascão, which marks the border with the Alentejo.

8. **(18km)** The road wiggles upwards on the other side of the river, climbing gently for about 5km.

The scenery then starts to open out a lot, with the trees becoming more scattered and the slopes much more gentle.

Note: This is an area that can look beautiful in early spring when the fields are green and covered with wildflowers.

From summer through into winter, though, it can look extremely harsh, with the grass dried to next to nothing and the bare soil clearly visible.

There's a **café** in the hamlet of Dugueno but nowhere else to stop along this section.

After the climb up from the river, the road becomes more undulating again as the N2 continues roughly north-westwards.

Coming into Almodôvar, the N2 passes a junction with the N267 from Mertola and then curves to the left and crosses a bridge.

Follow the road up into town and at the top of the hill you come to a left turn, sandwiched between banks on each corner and signposted 'Salir-Loulé'.

The centre of town and the market are off to the left here.

OVERNIGHT: ALMODÔVAR

Almodôvar (pop 7,500) is a typical Alentejean town, with a cluster of old streets in the middle, surrounded by some more modern developments. There's a small market just off Rua Serpa Pinto in the centre of town.

The town lies close to the edge of the Alentejo plains with the hills of the Serra do Caldeirão (and the border with the Algarve region) to the south. There are no particular sights but it's a pleasant enough place and its streets aren't as narrow as some other towns in the region.

From here, you can also ride to Mertola to the east (42.1km), Castro Verde to the north (21.6km) or Odemira to the west (80.9km) – for more details see Pedal Portugal's guidebook for *The Alentejo Circuit*.

Historically, the town was once famous for its cobblers and one rather quirky feature to spot is the sculpture on a roundabout on the north-east of town (off Rua António Cândido Colaço).

The 10m-high cobbler is made entirely from scrap metal – old sewing machines hold an apron made of giant circular saw blades.

Supermarkets

There's a Pingo Doce on the N393 going out to Ourique. There's also a Minipreço on the left if you go a short distance north of the centre on the N2.

Accommodation

Camping:

There is no campsite anywhere in the immediate area.

Hotels & Guest Houses:

Camões, Rua A. do Maldonado 11F, 7700-012 Almodôvar. *Tel:* 286 665 150. *Web:* atcamoes.com.pt

Hotel Serafim (2*), Rua do Afonso 9, 7700-053 Almodôvar *Tel:* 286 660 010 *Email:* residencialserafim@mail.telepac.pt *Web:* hotelserafim.pt

Corvos e Cadvais, Estrada N2, km 661, 7700-016 Almodôvar
Tel: 966 170 769 *Email:* info@corvosecadavais.pt
Web: corvosecadavais.pt

For other options, take a look at:
cm-almodovar.pt/directorio/vila/

DAY TWO: ALMODÔVAR – LOULÉ

Overview

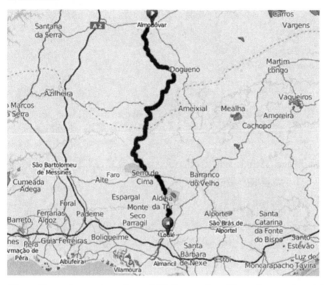

Overall you're going downhill from the Alentejo to the Algarve on this ride – but it might not feel like it.

The route is quite simple, going roughly due south and with only about four junctions along the way.

Most of the ride is through hill country, some of it farmed but most of it a mixture of wild-looking scrub and forestry.

The first 26km are undulating but generally climbing to the first of two mountain ridges you need to cross. After reaching a height of 530m, you've then got about 5km of mostly downhill before starting the ascent to the second ridge.

This is Malhão, the summit that features in the *Volta ao Algarve* professional road race. After going past the Buddhist stupa near the top (yes, really), you've then got a very steep (over 19% in one place) descent towards Salir.

There are a couple more moderate climbs on the way to Loulé but it's downhill into the town at the end.

Be warned that there few **cafés** or other stops on the 46km between Almodôvar and Salir.

Stats

Distance: 61.3km
Total elevation gain: +995m/-1103
Maximum incline: 10.6%

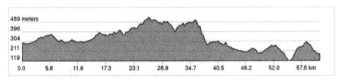

To download a map with full ride profiles, available as .gpx file etc., see: ridewithgps.com/routes/7554849

Alternative routes

The only other option is to miss out the detour south of Curvatos and keep going along the M1198/Cidadãos road towards Malhão.

This will save about 5km in distance and 30m of climbing.

DIRECTIONS: ALMODÔVAR – LOULÉ

1. **(600m)** From the junction on the N2 where the ride from Loulé finished, turn left onto Rua do Mercado, signposted 'Salir-Loulé'.

   Follow the road past the market on the right and the church on the left.

   Curve left around the back of the church and then fork right into Rua Serpa Pinto. Keep going until you get to a small roundabout.

2. **(8.9km)** Go straight on (second exit), signposted 'S. Barnabé', 'Salir/Loulé' and 'A2 Lisboa/Faro'.

   You're soon out into countryside on the M1198/Cidadãos road and riding roughly south-westwards through an area of small fields and olive trees.

   As the road turns to the south, this is replaced by larger fields of pasture/grazing dotted with cork oak trees.

   The first couple of kilometres are more or less flat, after which the road begins to climb but only in a gentle fashion.

It's about 3.5km to the top of the hill but you only ascend about 80m and then there's an equally gentle downhill on the other side into wilder-looking country.

About 1km past the hamlet of Curvatos you come to a turning on the left.

3. **(4.9km)** Turn left, signposted directions include 'Dogueno' and 'Cumeada'.

   The road is gently undulating for the next 5km, passing through a beautiful area of peaceful farmland with hardly any houses to be seen other than at the tiny hamlet of Azinhal.

   After running roughly south-east, the road comes up to a T-junction.

4. **(11.6km)** Turn right, signposted 'Corte Figueira' and 'Mendonça'.

   From here, the road climbs a little as it heads towards a small hamlet called Monte das Cumeadas and then becomes more twisting and undulating as it heads into hillier country.

   There's a basic **café/bar** in the next village of Corte

Figueira – look for the Taberna a Forja on the right just before the recycling bins.

The road bends to the left (south) just after the village and begins to climb from here, ascending about 290m over the course of the next 5.2km through some stunning scenery.

The top of the climb brings you to a T-junction back on the M1198/Cidadãos road.

5. **(9.5km)** Turn left, signposted 'Loulé' and 'Salir'. Unless it's been relaid recently, the surface along this next section is much rougher (another reason for taking the previous detour).

It's a rolling ride across the hills for the next 4km – thankfully coming on to a newer section of surface.

The road then drops to a bridge over a small valley that marks the Alentejo-Algarve border.

From here, the climb begins to Malhão (just over 100m of ascent spread over about 4km). The first section is by far the worst and after that it's mostly quite gentle and more undulating.

As you come up towards the top, you pass a petrol station on the right and then a **café** just off the road at the crest of the hill. This is a favourite spot with local cyclists who have done the climb from the other side, particularly at weekends.

Across the road a track leads to an unusual site for Portugal, a Tibetan Buddhist stupa. (See page 142.)

6. **(9.9km)** From the junction by the café, the road swings to the left (paralleling the track to the stupa) then starts to descend fast.

This is by far and away the steepest part of the ride. The first section reaches a gradient of just over 13% but that's just the start. You get a bit of respite from the braking as the road levels out a bit going around a hairpin bend.

The next section, is even steeper, hitting 19.2%. In total, the downhill from Malhão descends about 225m over 2.4km – an average incline of 9.1%.

You're also advised to watch out for the really tight left-hand hairpin bend at the very bottom of the hill!

Once you're down, there's a moderate climb for about 1km across a small ridge of hills to where the road becomes the M503. From here, it's then downhill for the next 6km all the way to a T-junction on the N124.

Note: The ride south of the foot of Malhão takes you through thickly wooded hills.

As you approach the N124, off to your right is a protected area around some limestone cliffs known as the **Rocha da Pena**.

There are walks here as well as opportunities to spot the local flora and fauna, including lots of birds. (See page 162.)

7. **(2.4km)** Turn left on the N124, signposted 'Loulé', and enjoy 1.2km of riding on the flat.

    That will bring you to a roundabout where you need to turn right on the M525 towards Salir (signposted 'Loulé'.)

    There's a bit of a climb up to the village, where there are a couple of **cafés** and several turnings into the old part of the village, which is on the hill to the left.

The road levels off as it approaches the last turning back into the centre.

Note: There are the ruins of a small castle at the top of the hill, in the centre of the village. There's not a lot to see but it's a pretty spot with good views of the surrounding countryside.

8. **(10.9km)** From Salir, the M525 descends into an area of pleasant countryside. Part of this section is narrow so watch out for other traffic, although this isn't a main route so rarely gets too busy.

    After about 6.9km you come to a set of traffic lights at a crossroads with the M524. Go straight on and then across a bridge over the Ribeira de Algibre.

    It's fairly flat for a few hundred metres after the bridge but then you start the last serious climb of the day – and the steepest.

    Over the next 3km, the M525 ascends around 162m, reaching a maximum gradient of 10.6% (although the average over the hill is only 5.8%). The first 1km of hill is also the worst, after that it gets much more gentle and the incline stays quite steady. There's also a good surface and a decent shoulder most of the way.

At the top of the hill, there are some houses where the road curves to the left and then does a 90° right turn.

9. **(2.6km)** Follow the M525 to the right – it's downhill from here all the way into Loulé.

It gradually gets more built-up as you descend the hill but it's a reasonable road with a shoulder on both sides and will bring you to a roundabout on a fairly new road that bypasses the north of the city.

Go straight across the roundabout (second exit) and then take the right fork in the road where it becomes one-way.

Keep going until you come to a T-junction on Rua de Nossa Senhora de Fátima. Turn left and continue until you come to a set of traffic lights at a crossroads. (You should see the entrance to the city's park to the left.)

Turn right into Avenida 25 de Abril (the N396), which will bring you down to the roundabout that marks the start and end of the Almodôvar Loop.

Hunkara Dzong stupa

Opposite the junction by the café at the top of Malhão is a track marked by a green flag. If you walk a couple of hundred metres along it this takes you to a very incongruous sight in Portugal – a Tibetan Buddhist stupa or shrine.

Consecrated in October 2008, the six-metre high monument was carved out of grey-rose granite quarried in Portugal and is designed to represent the Buddha's enlightenment.

Prayer flags flutter in the wind around the stupa and, even if you're not affected by any religious feelings, it's a beautiful and very peaceful spot to admire the view, which stretches all the way to the Atlantic.

A short distance from the stupa, a collection of associated low-rise buildings belongs to the Association of World Peace, a group set up following the teachings of the Tibetan Buddhist tradition.

For more information see: stupapaznomundo.org/home-en

MAPS: ALMODÔVAR LOOP

21. Querenca

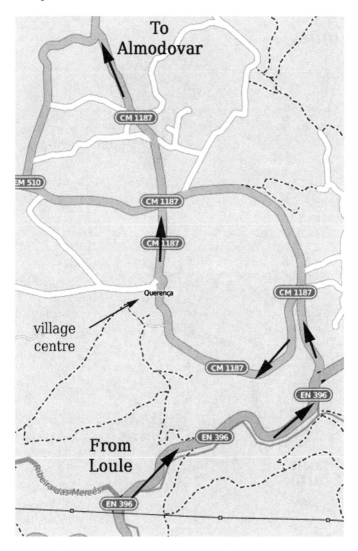

22. Almodôvar

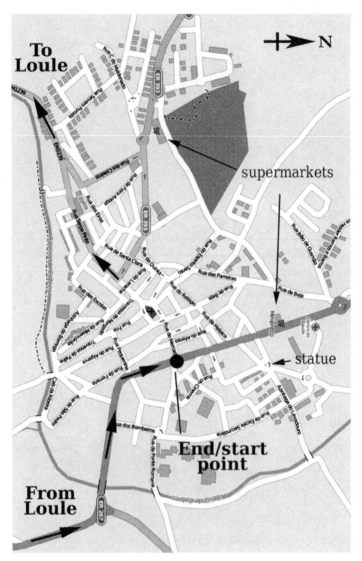

For **Loulé**, see Map 16 on page 123.

DAY RIDES

Whether you're looking for a gentle spin for a few hours or something a bit tougher, this section contains a variety of rides to get you on your way.

Day rides are listed under the name of the town that acts as the start/finish point. They include:

- **Aljezur** – two rides: 14.9 and 30km
- **Boliqueime** – one ride: options from 44.8 to 73.7km
- **Lagos** – two rides/three options: 29.9, 32.7 or 58.1km
- **Mexilhoeira Grande** – two rides: 6 or 16.4km
- **Monchique** – one ride: 17.3km
- **Silves** – one ride: options for 46 or 59.5km
- **Zambujeira** – one ride: 47km

Each ride is introduced by a short overview that gives an idea of what's involved.

This is followed by a set of detailed directions and an outline map, with a link to an online route map, downloadable as a .gpx file etc..

How long?

I haven't given time estimates for any of the rides. That's because how long each one takes will vary enormously depending on a number of variables, including personal fitness, your bike, the number of stops, head/tailwinds, the heat, etc..

Hopefully the distances and description of what's involved will enable you to estimate how long you need to allow.

Let the train take some of the strain

To help get you to the start of as many rides as possible, a number begin from stations on the Faro-Lagos railway line. This regional service takes bikes for free, has a large guard's van in which to carry them and is cheap to use.

To check times and prices, see: cp.pt/passageiros/en/train-times

Extra options

You might also want to look at the stages featured in the main touring circuit. Parts of these rides could provide additional 'there and back' options.

ALJEZUR

There are two day rides below taking you out to see some of the area's beautiful beaches and coastal scenery – a relatively tough **30km circuit** visiting Monte Clerigo and Arrifana, and an almost flat **14.9km** there-and-back ride to Praia da Arrifana.

MONTE CLERIGO AND ARRIFANA

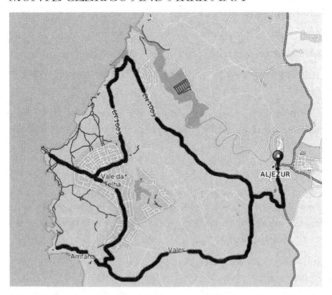

The 30km circuit below offers a chance to visit some dramatic cliffs and popular surfing beaches. However, it does involve a couple of stiff climbs, ascending from sea level to around 100m (330ft).

The beaches here are very popular with both surfers and other visitors, particularly at weekends and in the summer months.

Because of this, you may have to contend with a reasonable number of cars on relatively narrow roads. Having said that, visibility on the route is mostly good.

Some of the area around Arrifana is spoilt by sprawling holiday developments – some seemingly placed at random on the hillside – but it's worth putting up with them for the views the rest of the way.

The circuit starts where the N120 crosses the bridge over the Ribeira de Aljezur immediately below the old town. There's a café right next to the bridge and plenty of parking on the other side of the river.

Stats

Distance: 30km
Total elevation gain: +/-437m
Maximum incline: 11.2%

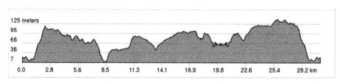

To download a map with full ride profile, available as .gpx file etc., see: ridewithgps.com/routes/7491464

Directions

1. **(1.1km)** Head south on the N120 until you see the brown signs indicating the turn for Monte Clerigo and Arrifana.

2. **(1.2km)** Turn right – and get in a low gear. This is the toughest climb, which is why there are two lanes for ascending vehicles, luckily also meaning more room for panting cyclists.

3. **(6km)** Turn right at the T-junction – you're at the top here and the road follows the ridge with the valley of the Ribeira de Aljezur down to the right.

Most of the land here is scrub until you come to a villa development on the right.

The road starts to drop towards the coast and comes

to a steep left-hand bend. A track to the right leads to some spectacular cliffs and sea views but there's no easy way down to the beach.

Swoop down into Monte Clerigo – but watch out for deep sand where the road crosses the top of the beach.

There's a **restaurant** and a **snack bar** next to the car park, with some colourful little houses and a boardwalk leading to the beach.

4. **(2.7km)** From Monte Clerigo, turn back inland. The road climbs again as it crosses an area of open hillside but not as steeply as before.

Just after a right-hand bend, the road reaches a roundabout.

5. **(2.5km)** From the roundabout it's about 2.5km out to a dramatic cape with fantastic views of cliffs and a sandy beach below the cliffs.

Go straight across the first roundabout, right at the next one and straight on at a third.

Unless it's been surfaced recently, the section from the third roundabout is unsealed so you may want to skip this or walk the 1.9km there and back.

6. **(6.6km)** The next section takes you out to the ruins of a small fort above the surf beach at Arrifana.

Return to the second roundabout and go straight ahead. Bear right when you come to a triangular green.

Keep going across another couple of roundabouts – follow brown signs for Arrifana.

You'll come to a T-junction at Praia de Arrifana. Turn right to ride up and out to the fort, from where you can look down on the incredible beaches to the south.

The surf here can be spectacular and this is a very popular beach, with a couple of hairpin roads going down the cliff.

There are several **cafés** and **restaurants** along the road out here, as well as a **youth hostel**.

7. **(7.6km)** From the fort, retrace your steps and just keep going along the same road, the M1003-1, for 7.6km.

This will bring you round to the top of the first big hill

out of Aljezur and you return the same way as on leaving the town.

Note: On the way down the hill, a small side road goes off to the left at the first bend. If you turn off this will take you along a ridge to the ruins of Aljezur's castle.

However, the final section down into the town is extremely steep and cobbled so you may prefer to return the way you came.

Maps

See **6: Aljezur** on page 57 and **23: Arrifana** on page 196.

PRAIA DA AMOREIRA

If you fancy a shorter trip out to the beach from Aljezur, an alternative option is a **14.9km** there-and-back ride out to the Praia da Amoreira.

This is the beach at the mouth of the Aljezur river (which can be seen from the road out to Monte Clerigo) and it's another wide expanse of sand with some jagged cliffs to the north.

Be warned, however, that most of the road out to Amoreira is very rough and badly in need of resurfacing – except for the very last section, which is beautifully smooth.

Stats

Distance: 14.9km
Total elevation gain: +/-205m
Maximum incline: 9.8%

To download a map with full ride profile, available as .gpx file etc., see: ridewithgps.com/routes/7496890

Directions

To get here, the simplest way is to head straight north along the cobbled roads of Aljezur's old town – just keep the river on your right.

Take a right on a sealed road as you leave the town behind and this will take you over the river.

Once across the bridge turn left and just keep going to the beach.

If you don't want to ride over the cobbles in the old town, simply follow the N120 north out of town, back towards Odeceixe. The turn for Amoreira is signposted off on the left next to the town's *complexo desportivo* (sports centre).

Maps

See **6: Aljezur** on page 57 and **23: Arrifana** on page 196.

BOLIQUEIME (STATION)

Boliqueime is a large village about 8km inland from the coast, lying roughly midway between Albufeira and Loulé. The train station here is a good jumping off point for rides into the countryside immediately to the north and the hills beyond.

ALTE AND CALDEIRÃO FOOTHILLS

The ride below provides several opportunities for loops of various length, riding through small villages, orange groves, farmland, and the foothills of the Serra do Caldeirão.

One stop is Alte, which some local tourist literature calls the prettiest village in Portugal. That's probably taking things a bit far but it certainly is an attractive, if touristy, place.

Road-wise, there are a few sections (such as around Alte) that might get busy in the main holiday season or at weekends but most of the route is on quiet country roads and back lanes.

The longest – and toughest – option takes you on a **73.7km circuit** to the north and east of Boliqueime.

However, there are several opportunities to shorten the ride – and cut out some of the worst hills. See page 159 for the **43.5km shorter option**.

The long version is a reasonably tough ride. There's approaching 1,100m of climbing involved over the circuit. None of it is excessive – the maximum incline is just over 11%, although there are a few other sections that are almost this steep.

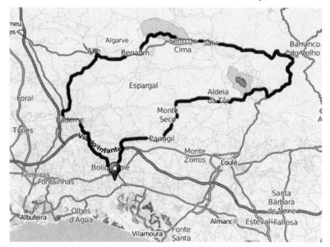

The short version is a lot gentler, although still involving some hills. Total ascent is 690m and the steepest incline just over 10%.

The main description below is for the full circuit, notes after this explain where and how to shorten the ride.

The ride starts from the north (inland) side of Boliqueime station. Be warned that the first 2.5km involves some fairly steady climbing – although it does get easier after that.

Stats

Distance: 73.7km   *Total elevation gain:* +/-1131
Maximum incline: 12.2%

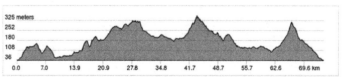

To download a map with full ride profile, available as .gpx file etc., see: ridewithgps.com/routes/7338478

Directions

1. **(1.2km)** Go left on the lane that runs parallel with the railway line. After about 100m this bends to the right and takes you to a crossroads on the main N125.

   Go straight across (blue signs for a *farmácia*) into Rua Nova. Keep going straight up the hill, ignoring turnings on the left and right and following the *farmácia* signs.

   It's a bit of a climb as you come up into the centre of Boliqueime, where there are various **cafés** as well as shops.

   Rua Nova comes to a crossroads on the main N270 road through the village.

2. **(7.8km)** Turn right here, still going uphill. The road's a bit rough and quite narrow but brings you up to an attractive plaza around the church.

   The N270 continues to climb for about 100m and then does an almost 90° turn to the right, signposted 'Paderne'. The road bends right back on itself and then turns north as it starts to leave the village behind.

The climbing does then slacken off and you're rewarded with some excellent views of the rolling hills and fields around you.

There's a nice downhill of about 2km as you come down through some wilder hills and cross under the A22 motorway.

Sadly another hill follows but this one is only just over a 1km in length and the scenery along here is all very pretty: small fields with stone walls, almond trees and olives, white and pastel-painted houses and a couple of sleepy villages.

Its then downhill again all the way into Paderne, where the N270 brings you down to a car park at the bottom of town. (There are public **toilets** off to the left beyond the health centre building – which looks like a bungalow with a large veranda.)

Note: Paderne looks fairly scruffy on the way through but has some cobbled back streets to wander if you want a break.

If you turn right by the church and follow the cobbled street that runs parallel with the N270 there are several **cafés**, as well as a post office and a small **supermarket**.

3. **(1.4km)** From the bottom of Paderne, the N270 goes downhill and across the Ribeira de Quarteria then turns to the right as it goes through the wonderfully named hamlet of Purgatório.

Keep going north to the first right turn, signposted 'Alcaria'.

4. **(7.8km)** Turn right here, on to the M1174. This is a lovely quiet lane that wiggles its way across level fields and past various smallholdings and farms.

Keep following the narrow street through the white-painted houses of Alcaria and then head on north, riding past fruit trees, spiky agave plants and small patches of vines.

Go straight on at the stop sign where the M1174 meets the M1173 and then straight on again at the next junction, signposted 'Monte Brito' and 'Alte'.

After just over 4km, the road starts to turn to the north-east and climb gently. Monte Brito is a strung-out collection of low-rise buildings where the road

again narrows. After bending to the right in the village, the M1174 then makes a sharp left past a small bougainvillea-decked **café**.

The climbing gets a bit steadier and steeper after this, going up to an incline of almost 10% in one part.

It gets gentler again as you come to the top of the ridge – and then you can see the next valley with Alte on the other side.

You lose about 50m in height going down into the valley, which unfortunately you have to regain to come up (another reasonably steep climb) to a T-junction on the N124 just to the east of Alte.

5. **(1.1km)** Turn left on the N124 towards Alte. After 270m, take the first right – there are a number of signs, including a brown sign for the *Fontes* (springs).

Follow the road gently up for another 350m. Then take the first left and turn left again in about 50m.

Note: If you turn right here instead, this is Rua da Fonte, which will take you up a small valley to the two springs.

The first one, Fonte Pequena, has a restaurant in an old mill. There's a **picnic area** under the trees next to the mill.

> After turning left, head towards the centre of Alte on Rua da Fonte. Keep to the right at the next fork in the road then take the second turning on the left.

> This street will take you down to the back of the church. Follow it around the building and down to the main street.

Note: There are plenty of **cafés** and **restaurants** around the centre of Alte catering to the tourist trade – and it can be heaving here when the tour buses arrive.

Standing with your back to the church, there are public **toilets** down an alleyway to the right next to the *junta de freguesia* (council offices).

About 100m along on the left (opposite the tiny covered **market**) steps lead down to a small **supermarket**.

6. **(6km)** From the centre of Alte, continue down past the covered market. Keep going straight on until you come to a roundabout on the N124.

Turn left here (third exit) and follow the road back around the bottom of the village towards the junction where you first turned off into Alte.

Keep following the N124, past where you came up from Paderne, and continue east.

The road climbs for the next couple of kilometres then levels off and becomes more rolling, heading east through parched-looking hill country, with areas of citrus and almond trees and good views off to either side.

There's a bit of a downhill as you come into the village of Benafim Grande.

Note: If you're looking for a **café** take the third turning on the left, with the blue sign and red cross indicating the *centro da saude* (health centre).

> Otherwise, continue to a junction where the N124 curves to the left and a right turn goes off straight ahead.

Note: For anyone taking the shorter option on this ride, this is where you need to turn right (straight on) – following signposts for 'Alta Fica', 'Loulé' and 'Faro'.

See the **Shorter Option** section below for details of this route.

7. **(3km)** Keep going on the N124 to a roundabout, where you turn left. This takes you up out of the village on a country lane, following it around to the right at the top of the hill.

Straight ahead you can see the **Rocha da Pena** (see page 162), an important wildlife reserve.

The road (the M1094) continues north-east and goes up into the hamlet of Penina, where you go past a bus stop on the left and turn right into a tiny street.

You're soon back into the countryside, riding past small fields. After about 400m you pass through a small group of houses and come to a left turn – with a brown signpost to the Rocha da Pena.

8. **(1.3km)** Turn left here. The road climbs for a short distance and then turns roughly east to follow the hillside.

You will come to a small **café**, which is next to the start of a walk up to Rocha da Pena.

9. **(4.9km)** From the café, head south-east and down the hill at a 45° angle. After about 2.8km, you will come to a T-junction on the M503.

Turn right here – signposted 'Silves', 'Loulé' and 'Alte' - and follow the road back to the N124.

Turn left towards Loulé and continue to the next roundabout.

Note: If you turn right at the roundabout, the village of Salir is not far up the hill.

There's a small *supermercado* (**supermarket**) and a *pastelaria* (**bakery**) and **café** in about 800m, plus some pretty cobbled streets around the ruins of a small castle higher up.

This junction also gives another opportunity for a **shorter ride**. If you take the M525 south from Salir, it's just over 6km to a crossroads on the M524 where you rejoin the main circuit at **Point 13**. This shortcut reduces the distance to just under **61km**.

10. **(8.6km)** For the longer circuit, continue straight on at the roundabout on the N124.

There's a short hill then the road descends through some beautiful countryside for about 3km. After another short climb you've got another 2km that's relatively flat.

Then, however, the climbing starts with the N124 ascending from about 200m to about 360m in altitude.

As it enters an area of wooded hills, the road starts to twist and turn. However, none of the inclines on this section are that severe – it's all below 10% and most is more like 5-8%.

The first junction you come to is a right turn onto the N396.

11. **(7km)** Turn right – signposted 'Loulé'. The road continues eastwards and climbs for about another 1.5km before it turns south-east and starts to descend.

It's a lovely run down from here almost all the way to Querença, dropping around 180m in height through thickly forested hills on a quiet road.

After about 5.5km of downhill, you will see a right turn, signposted 'Tôr',

'Querença' and 'Fonte de Benémola'.

12. **(5.7km)** Turn right on the M524, which climbs for about 1km as it heads north before levelling off. The road then descends again as it turns west and takes you around Querença.

There's a good smooth surface as the M524 drops down and skirts around the southern edge of the Fonte de Benémola nature reserve – a large wooded area with a natural spring in its centre (see **Note** below).

The road turns south as it follows the Ribeira de Benémola. The valley gets flatter and more open – and turns to the west – as the Benémola joins another stream and becomes the Ribeira de Algibre.

The next couple of kilometres remain fairly smooth and level, bringing you to a set of traffic lights at a crossroads with the M525.

Note: There's a car park just off the M524 on the edge of Fonte de Benémola reserve. It's a fairly gentle one-and-a-half hour stroll around the area on a walking trail that goes off from here.

For more information, see: algarvewildlife.com/walksc-benemola.php

13. **(5.5km)** Go straight across at the lights (right if coming from Salir), sticking on the M524. The road continues along the Algibre valley. There are a few houses and you'll see far more olive trees than people (or cars).

The ride is slightly undulating but remains almost on the level, descending slightly to a T-junction.

14. **(3.8km)** Turn left on the M524-1, signposted 'Loulé'. The road turns roughly south and crosses the river – after which it starts to climb steadily.

This is the warm-up for the last big climb of the circuit. The gradient is all pretty gentle as you head up the south side of the valley and into the hills.

There are a few small orchards along the way but most of the scenery is wild and unspoilt. The climb gets slightly steeper as you head up through a couple of small villages but is still only about 5.5%.

As you come to the top of a rise in the village of Paragil, there's a crossroads next to some blue and white-painted buildings, with minor roads going off to either side.

There are also a couple of basic **cafés** to either side of this crossroads.

Note: If you've had enough climbing and want to avoid Picota (the steep hill coming up), you can go straight on here – in which case see **Point 8** in the directions for the shorter version of this route (but also see the note regarding the N270 in the introduction).

15. **(3km)** Turn right on the M1177. The road keeps climbing, gently at first but soon getting steeper as it heads up a sharp little hill called Picota.

The views are fantastic but it's 1km to the top with the incline reaching almost 11% before you get there.

Once you've made it to the summit of Picota, though, the good news is that it's downhill literally all the way to the end of the ride.

It's a gorgeous run down from the top, steep at first

but gradually getting more gentle.

Coming down into the village of Corga you come to a small crossroads with a metal wheel above an old well on your right.

16. **(4.6km)** Turn right here on to the M1181, signposted 'Tenoca'. The road continues gently downhill. It's also all very rural with olive and orange trees beside the road.

Coming down into Tenoca, you reach a kind of staggered crossroads. Turn left, signposted 'Fonte de Boliqueime'. You're still on the M1181.

It's slightly more built-up around here but still very pretty as you head down under the A22 motorway, continuing downwards and roughly southwards.

The descent is quite gentle now (only around 2%) but it's easy riding all the way down to Boliqueime.

As you come into the village, the road curves right by a pink house and then almost immediately comes to a T-junction.

17. **(1km)** Turn left and follow the road for 300m to a double roundabout at a junction of the N125 and the N270.

Go right to join the N270 at the first roundabout and then, after stopping at the traffic lights, take the second exit on the next one – signposted *estacão* (station).

This is the N125-3 and takes you on a straight line back to the station and the end of the ride.

Maps

See **24: Boliqueime** (page 197) and **21: Querenca** (page 125).

ALTE AND CALDEIRÃO FOOTHILLS – SHORTER OPTION

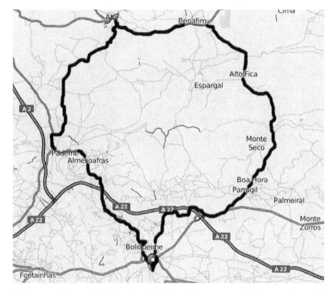

This version of the circuit is still reasonably tough, taking in Paderne, Alte and Benafim Grande before turning back towards Boliqueime.

However, it does avoid the two biggest climbs on the longer circuit: the 5km ascent going east on the way to Querença and the steep climb to Picota at the end.

The only negative aspect is that avoiding Picota means riding for 1.4km on the N270. This is a reasonably busy road and goes past a large quarry and you have to watch out for trucks on this section.

However, this is a downhill section with good visibility (no real bends) so should be reasonably safe.

If you don't want to chance the main road, you can still go via Picota, which although quite a lot hillier, is only 100m further. To do so, see the end of **Point 14** in the longer route above.

Stats

Distance: 44.8km
Total elevation gain: +/-716m
Maximum incline: 10%

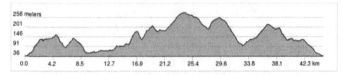

To download a map with full ride profile, available as .gpx file etc., see: ridewithgps.com/routes/7338539

Directions

For the first part of this ride, follow **Points 1-6** above.

7. **(6.8km)** Turn right (going straight ahead) on the M524-2, signposted 'Alta Fica', 'Loulé' and 'Faro'.

   After 350m, the road bends right and heads south-east, going down the side of the valley at a 45° angle.

   After that lovely steady downhill the road starts to climb again. The incline reaches 9.9% on this section but it's a good road surface and most of it's quite a lot more gentle.

   It's less than 1km to the top of the hill. After that, the road runs more or less flat for about 500m before a last gentle little climb to the village of Alto Fica.

   From this point the road becomes the M524 – and it's downhill again all the way to the junction with the M524-1 in the Algibre valley.

8. **(4.4km)** Go straight on at this junction – which is where the longer version of this route comes in on the way back from Querença.

   The road crosses the Ribeira de Algibre – and then starts to climb steadily.

   However, the gradient is all pretty gentle as you head up the south side of the valley and into the hills.

   There are a few small orchards along the way but most of the scenery is wild and unspoilt. The climb gets slightly steeper as you head through a couple of small villages but is still only about 5.5%.

As you come to the top of a rise in Paragil, there's a crossroads next to some blue and white-painted buildings, with minor roads to either side. There are also a couple of basic **cafés** to either side.

Go straight on here (or right if you want to go via Picota –see **Point 15** on page 157) for about another 100m as the road runs, more or less level, through Paragil.

9. **(1.4km)** Turn right, signposted 'Matos Picota', on to the M1191, which takes you south-west on a gentle downhill to a T-junction on the N270.

10. **(1.4km)** Turn right on the main road, which climbs slightly for about 100m as it passes the first entrance to a large quarry. It's very dusty around here and there are trucks going in and out so take care on this section.

Just past the quarry entrance, the N270 starts to descend, bending slightly to the right as it takes you past another quarry gateway.

As you come down the hill the N270 does a 90° bend to the left and you'll see a right-turn lane just before a petrol station.

11. **(1.1km)** Turn off the N270 here, signposted 'Tenoca' and 'Campina', on the M1180, which climbs very slightly, taking you on to a lovely quiet rural road.

After about 650m, as the road comes towards a small group of houses, there is an unsignposted left turn.

Turn here, which will take you over the A22 motorway and south on a well-sealed lane. In about 450m, you come to a small crossroads.

12. **(1.2km)** Turn right on a pretty, single-track lane that runs west through fields and orchards, going past a number of smallholdings.

After a sharp right-hand bend, the road goes up a small hill for about 100m and then turns hard left. Keep going for another 600m until you come to a T-junction on the M1181.

13. **(2.2km)** Turn left on to the M1181, now on the same route as the longer circuit coming down from Picota.

From here it's a gentle descent (about 2%) and easy riding all the way down to Boliqueime.

As you come to the village, the road curves right by a pink house and then comes to a T-junction.

14. **(1km)** Turn left and follow the road for 300m to a double roundabout at a junction of the N125 and the N270.

15. Go right to join the N270 at the first roundabout and then, after stopping at the lights, take the second exit on the next one, signposted *estacão* (station).

This is the N125-3 and takes you on a straight line back to the station and the end of the ride.

Maps

See **24: Boliqueime** (see page 197).

Rocha da Pena

This is a beautiful area of limestone pavement and karst formations popular with wildlife enthusiasts and climbers.

Four-legged wildlife found here includes the genet, wild boar and mongoose, while the bird life includes lots of raptors, warblers and woodpeckers.

The area's also famous for a Neolithic wall, endangered bats, amazing views and huge numbers of bird and flower species.

If you do decide to get off your bike and take a look, be warned that the café is at an altitude of about 315m and the top of the hill reaches almost 480m.

For more information on the site and its wildlife, see: algarvewildlife.com/walksc-rochadapena.php

LAGOS (STATION)

Lagos is a good base for exploring the Algarve's far west and there's some gorgeous riding to the north and west of town.

The resort villages immediately are a bit built up and can get busy in season. However, there are some stunning beaches all along the coast between Lagos and Sagres at the south-western tip of Portugal.

Inland, the landscape is mostly quite unspoilt and provides some good quiet roads, although it gets progressively more rugged the further away from the coast you go.

To the east, the Alvor estuary (and Portimão beyond) mean there are limited cycling options in this direction.

The town is quite hilly. It's also more built up and busy on the west side, meaning the best cycling routes tend to all go out to the north and north-east.

There are two rides described below – both start from Lagos railway station, which is on the opposite side of the river from the old town, next to the marina from where a footbridge crosses into the centre.

The first ride comprises two loops – giving you the option for a **29.9km circuit** into the countryside or a **58.1km double loop** that also takes in a lovely section of coast.

The second is a **32.7km ride** into the edge of the hills north of Lagos, climbing up to the dam on the Bravura reservoir.

See also Mexilhoeira Grande (page 176) for a 16.4km ride from the station there back to Lagos.

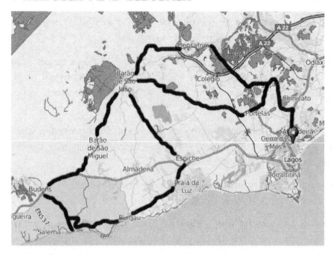

This ride is in two parts. One is a **29.9km circuit** going out to the north-west, visiting the villages of Bensafrim and Barão de São João and exploring some quiet country roads.

From Barão de São João, a second loop goes south-west, taking you to a couple of gorgeous beaches. Doing both loops together creates a kind of figure of eight with a total distance of **58.1km**.

Most of the riding on this circuit is fairly quiet and rural although there are busier sections leaving Lagos and on the return. There's also a brief section on the N125 further west but there's a wide shoulder and it's pretty safe.

There are a few hills, including a couple that are quite steep but also short.

The worst climb is on the second part of the figure of eight, leaving the beach at Boca do Rio (see page 78). This has a gradient of just over 17% but it's only short.

Either way, whether you pedal or walk, it shouldn't take too long to conquer and the views from the top are worth the effort.

Stats

Distance: 59km
Total elevation gain: +/-626m
Maximum incline: 17.2%

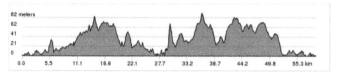

To download a map with full ride profile, available as .gpx file etc., see: ridewithgps.com/routes/7277305

Directions

1. **(950m)** Go north from the station along the back of the pink Marina de Lagos building and follow the road around to the right.

   Turn left at the roundabout (third exit) and follow the road to the junction on the main N125 Lagos-Portimão road.

2. **(1.3km)** Turn right on to the N125. Although this road is often busy, there is a wide shoulder that gives you room to cycle away from the traffic – and you're not on the road for very long.

   Keep going, past the petrol station and the aerodrome turning, to the next left turn.

3. **(4.1km)** Turn left, signposted 'Bensafrim' and 'Sargaçal', on the M535-1. The road heads roughly

north-east as it heads into the countryside and then turns to the north.

After about 2.4km the road does a sharp left. Another 500m further on, as you come into the village of Caldeiroa, the M535-1 then does a 90° turn right on a sharp little hill next to a **café**.

The hill is only about 300m long and then you've got a nice downhill to a T-junction on the N120.

4. **(4.7km)** Turn right on the N120, going north towards Bensafrim. Apart from the occasional bus or lorry, there's not a lot of heavy traffic on this road and it's nice and rural.

   Follow the main road over the Ribeira de Bensafrim

and up into the village. There's not a lot to see here but there are a couple of **cafés** on the right and another one at the far end of the village, near a **bakery** and small **market**.

The road climbs gently past the houses. Keep going until just before the sign marking the end of the village.

5. **(4.4km)** Turn left, signposted '*cemeterio novo*' and 'Hortinha'. You're now on a single-track country lane that wiggles its way west, past various smallholdings and country villas.

There are a few ups and downs but nothing major. After about 2km, the road turns south-west, running along the base of a line of scrub-covered hills to your right.

Keep going straight on until you come to a 'stop' sign by a small bridge with a T-junction on the other side. Turn left here and follow the road round towards the church and into Barão de São João.

Bear right at the church and this will bring you into a small plaza near the start of a cobbled, one-way street with a few **cafés** on it. You can go straight on (right) here and then left.

But for a smoother option go left in front of the church and follow the road around to the next T-junction.

Note: If you want to just ride the shorter 29.9km circuit, this is where you turn back. Take the left turn, signposted 'Lagos' and then follow the instructions from **Point 14** below.

6. **(6.2km)** Turn right, signposted 'Sagres'. Keep going straight, on what becomes the M535, heading south-west on a very gently rolling road, with the hills (topped with some big wind turbines) to your right.

The M535 turns more to the south as it heads towards the next village – Barão de São Miguel. There's not a lot to see in the village, although there is another **café** on a road going off to the right near the church.

From Barão de São Miguel the M535 zigzags slightly, with a few more fairly small hills on the way, as it heads towards a T-junction on the main N125 Lagos-Sagres road.

7. **(2.3km)** Turn right on the N125. This road can get busy – certainly in comparison with the other roads on this circuit. However, it's only really bad in peak holiday season or at weekends. There is also a good, wide shoulder so you should be well away from the traffic.

Follow the N125 towards Budens – there's an Intermarché **supermarket** (with bakery and café) on the right as you come to the village.

Keep going on the main road towards the end of the village, where there is a left turn with a brown sign for Boca do Rio.

8. **(2.9km)** Turn left here. Straight away you're on a quiet rural road that follows a valley dropping gently down to the south-east, getting wilder as it continues.

Just past a stand of big eucalyptus trees the valley opens out. Keep going straight on and the road will take you down to a parking area just above the beach at Boca do Rio (see page 78).

There are sometimes quite a lot of camper vans parked here but it's otherwise a very unspoilt and pretty spot.

9. **(5.4km)** Retrace your route back up the valley to the stand of eucalyptus trees and turn right here. The road loops back round to the other side of the river from the beach car park.

The hill beyond is the worst one on the circuit – with a maximum incline of just over 17%. However, it's not that long and the views are stunning. (If you can make it to the bend then you've conquered the worst of it.)

From here, the road continues into Burgau, joining the one-way system as you come into the village.

Note: There are several possible detours along this section.

The first is where a track goes off to the right at the top of the hill up from Boca do Rio. This leads to the **Forte de Almádena**. There's little left except for ruins but the fort is perched almost literally on the edge of the crumbling cliffs and offers incredible views along the coast.

About 800m further on there's another track on the right leading down to the beach at **Cabanas Velhas**. There's a seasonal beach café/restaurant here and more unspoilt beach lying beneath jagged cliffs. The beach curves around to the left, leading to a ruined harbour by the rocks at the point.

The third detour is in **Burgau** itself, which is a little touristy but very laid back compared to the resorts further east. The village also occupies a gorgeous setting up above another great beach and still retains a lot of its original charm.

Burgau also offers **cafés**, **restaurants** (many seasonal) and, if you need supplies, there's a **mini-mercado** on the right as you're leaving the village.

10. **(2.9km)** Turn right on to the one-way system and then keep left to follow the route on from Burgau.

The M537 gets more rural again as it takes you roughly north-east towards Luz.

The road bends to the right as it climbs a gentle hill. Before you get to the top, there's a small crossroads with holiday villa developments to both sides.

11. **(1.4km)** Turn left and head uphill through the villas then take the second turning on the right into Rua Longa.

Keep going up until you come to a T-junction at the top of the hill (with a small no through road opposite). Turn left here, continuing through an area of more low-rise villas set in large, private gardens.

The road curves to the right and then starts to descend, gradually getting more rural. About 750m from the top of the hill, the road starts to gently go back up and comes to a fork among some orchards of fig, almond and olive trees.

12. **(600m)** Turn right and continue for 200m until you get to the N125. If you want to stay on the tarmac, you need to turn right and then take the next left (in about 500m) for Espiche and then go 300m into the village.

Alternatively, on the other side of the N125 there's a short dirt track that joins the end of a small lane leading much more directly into the village. This leads through to a small plaza next to a chapel.

13. **(5.4km)** From the lane by the chapel, you want to take the middle of three roads going off to the left (north-west) – go past the café Palmeira and take the left fork.

The road looks a bit rough and narrow to begin with but soon takes you out into open countryside and starts to descend. Keep following this road and it will take you all the way back to the M535 just to the south-west of Barão de São João.

14. **(8.5km)** Turn right on the M535 and retrace your route back past Barão de São João. As you come to the end of the village, you pass the junction where you came down from the church.

Bear right here, signposted 'Lagos', on the M535-1. It's a rolling ride, past low scrubby hills and fields, quite a lot of them looking at least semi-abandoned.

After crossing the motorway link road between Lagos and the A22, the road goes over a small hill and then there's a lovely long downhill to the N120 and the Ribeira de Bensafrim.

15. **(6.2km)** Turn left on the N120 (away from Lagos) and then, in about 150m, take the next right on to a small lane.

Note: You can go right on the N120 for a more direct route to Lagos. However, there's a steep hill going this way – and a fairly narrow section on a bend with no hard shoulder.

This section of road can also be busy with local traffic at times, often going quite fast, and the route suggested below is probably a lot safer.

The lane zigzags around as it crosses the river and heads across some fields towards Caldeiroa, bringing you out next to the café on the steep bend that you passed near the start of the ride.

Go straight ahead at the junction by the café and retrace your route back to Lagos, returning to the T-junction on the N125, where you turn right.

Unfortunately the nice wide shoulder runs out (and is replaced with a pavement) just before the bridge over the Ribeira de Bensafrim estuary.

However, to return to the station, the simplest thing is to cross the road here.

It's not legal to make a left turn so you will need to walk across – watching carefully as traffic is often busy here.

Once across, rejoin the road opposite the car park for the Pingo Doce **supermarket**. At the next junction follow the road left, signposted 'Meia Praia'. Keep going past some apartment blocks to the next roundabout.

Turn right and follow the road around the back of the pink Marina de Lagos building. You'll see the train station ahead and to your left.

Note: If you don't want to risk crossing the N125, you will need to follow the road across the river and then around in a dual carriageway loop, over several roundabouts, to get to the riverfront in Lagos.

From here, you can take the pedestrian bridge over the river to the marina, with the train station straight ahead.

Maps

See **11: Lagos area** (page 79), **12: Lagos centre** (page 80) and **25: Lagos north** (page 198).

This ride is a **32.7km** trip exploring more of the countryside north of Lagos and going up into the edge of the hills to the dam on the Bravura reservoir.

The section going up to the dam itself is a there-and-back ride and there's one other bit in the middle that overlaps. However, around two-thirds of the ride is on different roads on the way out and on the return.

Although the ride involves climbing, most of it is fairly gentle. Overall, the total climb comes to 431m and most inclines are around 4-7%.

The steepest hill has a 9.5% incline but that's on the descent to the dam itself and you can always park at the café at the top and walk those few hundred metres.

The first few kilometres of this ride also leave Lagos on the same route as the **Villages and Beaches** ride above but after that you're into new territory – on quiet back roads that don't generally see much traffic.

Stats

Distance: 33km
Total elevation gain: +/-431m
Maximum incline: 9.5%

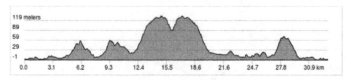

To download a map with full ride profile, available as .gpx file etc., see: ridewithgps.com/routes/7304168

Directions

1. **(1km)** Go north along the back of the pink Marina de Lagos building and follow the road around to the right.

   Turn left at the roundabout (third exit) and follow the road to the main N125 Lagos-Portimão road.

2. **(1.3km)** Turn right on the N125 – keeping on the wide shoulder to avoid the traffic.

   Keep going, past the petrol station and the aerodrome turning, to the next left turn.

3. **(2.4km)** Turn left, signposted 'Bensafrim' and 'Sargaçal', on the M535-1. The road heads roughly north-east into the countryside and then turns north.

   Just after a long white building on your left, the M535-1 does a sharp bend to the left (signposted 'Sargaçal') and another road goes off at 90° to the right.

4. **(1.9km)** Turn right, signposted 'Odiaxere'. The road climbs gently into a pretty landscape with fields to the left and trees to the right.

   The road dips down under one of the links from Lagos to the motorway then climbs up a small hill.

   As you start to descend towards the village of Odiaxere, you pass a bends sign. The road flattens out and a few hundred metres further on you come to a small, unsignposted crossroads.

5. **(700m)** Turn left onto a single-track lane. Follow it down a small hill and around

a bend to the right. The lane crosses an irrigation channel and goes down another section of hill, bends sharp left, and comes down to a T-junction on the N125-9.

6. **(1km)** Turn left on the N125-9 – this is a quiet two-lane road that heads towards some of the small villages in the hills and rarely gets much traffic. To begin with, as it follows the Ribeira de Odiaxere north-west, it's also pretty much flat then begins to climb very gently.

Just past a bus stop, with the motorway coming into view ahead, a small road forks off to the right.

7. **(3.1km)** Go right here on the M535, signposted 'Farta Vacas' (which I think translates as *abundant cows*) and 'Monte Ruivo'.

The lane climbs past a farm, goes under the A22 motorway and continues to go up for about another 300m before coming to the top of the ridge.

From here you get some good views of the rural scenery ahead and a nice downhill – even if the road surface is a bit rough in places.

As you come down to the hamlet of Monte Ruivo, the road does a 90° turn left and runs west before rejoining the N125-9 at another hamlet called Cotifo.

8. **(4.5km)** Turn right on the N125-9. In about 500m you pass a simple café on the right. A little further on there's a kind of crossroads.

Keep going straight on – there's a signpost for the 'Barragem' on the right.

From here it's a steady climb along a winding road up to the dam. The worst section of hill is about 1.5km long, reaching a maximum incline of just over 9%.

After that, the climb continues a little further but gets gentler as it ascends to a ridge and views of cistus-covered hills stretching into the distance.

The Bravura reservoir will come into view ahead, after which there's a downhill of about 500m towards the dam.

The road itself ends at the dam. On the other side there's a track that follows the edge of the reservoir if you fancy a walk, plus a network of forestry tracks going off into the hills.

Note: As you go down towards the dam, you will first come to a large car park with a small **café/snack bar** to one side. To avoid a steep return trip, you might want to leave your bike here and walk down – there's a footpath through the trees behind the café.

9. **(9.3km)** The first part of the return journey involves going back up the hill from the dam to the café (if you went down). From here you've got a lovely run down to the hamlet of Cotifo, where the road levels out again.

Do not turn off towards Monte Ruivo but follow the N125-9 straight on all the way back to Odiaxere.

As you come into the village, the road goes up a fairly steep but short hill, coming up to a pedestrianised area with a renovated traditional windmill to your left.

Keep going until you come to a T-junction on the main N125 Lagos-Portimão road.

10. **(2.7km)** Turn left on the N125 and then take the next right by a small plaza –

there's an orange signpost for the '*golfe*' course. The road then curves to the left and goes downhill, now signposted 'Palmares golfe' and 'Meia Praia'.

Follow the road down and round to the right and then up a short hill where the M510 curves to the left. There's a bit of a climb leaving the village but it soon evens out again.

You'll come to a T-junction where you turn right – following the same signposts.

About 200m further on, the road for the golf course and Meia Praia turns left. There's a bit of a climb here but this is the last hill of the day and is only about 750m long.

Before you get to the top of the hill, a new road goes off to the right.

Note: This road (although it's been in existence for a few years now) doesn't show up on any maps I've seen. It also doesn't appear if you use the maps on either Google Maps or Open Street Map but can be seen if you use the satellite view.

11. **(1.8km)** Turn right on the new road and follow it

around the edge of the golf course. It then comes down towards an area of new villa developments.

Before you get to the villas, though, you need to turn left on another new (and unmarked on maps) road that will take you down the hill to a roundabout just above the station at Meia Praia.

12. **(3km)** Turn right on the M534 beach road. This will take you back into Lagos past various apartment/holiday villa complexes.

Unfortunately there are a couple of (unnecessary) cobbled sections but luckily neither are that long.

Keep going straight on at the first roundabout. There is a large car park on the left before the next roundabout – which is where you came out from the marina area at the start of the ride.

Turn left here on to Rua Teixeira da Mota (with the Aparthotel Marina Club on your right) and follow the road back around the rear of the marina building and to the train station for the end of the ride.

Note: If you want to go into the centre of town, follow the road round to the right at the end of the marina building and go across the pedestrian bridge.

Maps

See **12: Lagos centre** (page 80), **25: Lagos north** (page 198) and **14: Odiaxere** (page 95).

MEXILHOEIRA GRANDE (STATION)

There are two options from this station – a **6km off-road ride** around the Alvor estuary and a **16.4km one way** journey to Lagos on back roads.

It's easy to get to Mexilhoeira by train – from Lagos it takes just 10 minutes and costs €1.40.

LAGOONS AND RIVER BEACHES

This short route is on gravel tracks rather than sealed roads but makes a nice gentle **6km loop** for when the weather's good. It also takes you into the *Reserva Natural da Ria do Alvor*, a protected area around this large estuary.

The mixture of lagoons, salt marshes and mudflats attracts a lot of bird life, including all kinds of waders (from flamingos to Portuguese clam fishermen). Inland, small rolling hills are covered by fields, copses and fruit/almond orchards.

The surface is reasonable for most of the way but it's probably best done only when the ground's good and dry. It also follows a marked walking trail (there's a signboard with a map on the north side of the railway line, next to the station) and the red and yellow *percurso pedestre* signs will help you follow your way.

The ride begins from the station – you can also add this as an extension to the Mexilhoeira-Lagos ride (see page 178).

Stats

Distance: 6km
Total elevation gain: +/-41m
Maximum incline: 5.7%

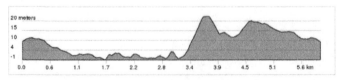

To download a map with full ride profile, available as .gpx file etc., see: ridewithgps.com/routes/7497028

Directions

1. **(350m)** Start from the track on the southern side of the station. Follow the track west, parallel with the railway line, until you come to a crossroads with a level crossing to the right.

2. **(2.4km)** Go straight ahead. The track curves a little to the left, running south-west past fields and a few smallholdings and houses.

   The track then does a 90° turn to the left where it comes to the edge of a large area of lagoons used for fish farming.

   It continues inland, turning to the south with areas of trees, fields and private houses up to the left and salt marshes to the right.

3. **(250m)** You will come to a junction with a track turning off and up a small hill to the left.

   Continue straight on and the track ends at a car park just back from a small, fairly sandy river beach.

   Note: Just beyond the junction mentioned above is a rough parking space on the right. The marked walking trail goes off here on a loop around an area of lagoon and salt marsh, coming back to the car park by the river beach.

   This loop of a little under 1.5km is probably not very practical for cycling but does provide a good opportunity for spotting some of the many water birds attracted to this spot.

4. **(2.6km)** Return to the previous junction and turn right, following the track up the hill and around to the left.

   There are good views from up here, looking north towards the Monchique hills and across the estuary towards Alvor and Portimão to the east.

   Keep following the track all the way back to the crossroads by the level crossing that you passed previously.

5. **(400m)** Turn right here to return to the station.

Maps

See **26: Mexilhoeira Grande** (page 199).

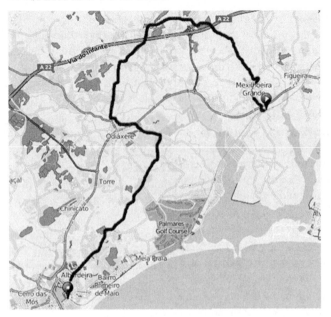

Zigzagging around to avoid busy roads, this **16.4km one-way** route takes you to Lagos through some quiet rural scenery.

There are a couple of small climbs but nothing major – the worst is going up south of Odiaxere to the hill above Meia Praia. Once you've got to the top, though, it's all downhill into Lagos.

Stats

Distance: 16.4km *Total elevation gain*: +163m/-169m
Maximum incline: 6.9%

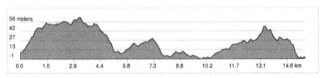

To download a map with full ride profile, available as .gpx file etc., see: ridewithgps.com/routes/7497153

Directions

1. **(200m)** From the station, turn left. Follow the road parallel with the railway and then around a bend to the right, taking you to a junction on the N125.

2. **(400m)** Cross the N125. Opposite and to the right is a small, unsignposted lane (Rua do Estacão) with a bridge over an irrigation channel.

   Follow the road up to a crossroads and go straight across. The road gets narrower as it goes up into the village but keep going, past turnings on either side, until you come to another crossroads.

3. **(550m)** You should see an arrow directing you to the right into a one-way street. Turn right here, past a couple of **cafés**, and follow the road up and around a bend to the left.

   Keep going straight on, passing various side roads, and follow the one-way signs as the road curves to the right.

   The road goes past a small **supermarket** on the right and another **café**. As you approach the church, take the right-hand fork and keep going up the hill until you come to a crossroads on the edge of the village.

4. **(2.9km)** Turn left and then take the next right in just under 100m on to the M1068, signposted 'Arão'.

   The road goes up a small hill with a white water tower on the right. You're soon into the countryside with excellent views ahead and to either side.

   The M1068 goes over the A22 motorway and then curves to the left, going roughly west until it comes to a new road raised up on an embankment straight ahead.

5. **(2.1km)** Turn right to run parallel with the new road; this is the link between the motorway and the Algarve International Autodrome (see page 93).

   The M1068 follows the autodrome road for about 450m before coming up to a roundabout.

   Go straight across (second exit). You now have to go back parallel with the autodrome road to rejoin the M1068's original route.

(Why they put the roundabout where they did is one of those bizarre bits of 'only in Portugal' engineering.)

Note: Online maps (Google and OpenStreetMap) show the M1068 going straight on through the autodrome road. It doesn't! You need to go up to the roundabout and back down the other side as described above.

The M1068 continues west past some small farms and private villas, before coming to a river, where it turns right and comes to a junction by a bridge.

6. **(1.5km)** Turn left over the bridge and then left again to follow the M539 south. Go up a gentle hill and under a large motorway flyover.

Immediately after the flyover, go past the start of a track and take the small lane going off at about 45° to the right.

Follow the lane for 800m until you come to a T-junction, where you turn right and then take the next left in less than 200m.

Note: There's a gravel track opposite the T-junction. You can go straight on here and cut the corner, missing out the left turn mentioned above.

7. **(1.6km)** Continue straight on towards Odiaxere, heading slightly east of south. As you come towards the village, the road crosses a small bridge, curves to the left and starts going uphill.

Part way up the hill is an old-fashioned well with a metal wheel on top.

8. **(800m)** Turn left here on to a slightly rough-looking back lane. This skirts the outside of the village, with houses up to your right and fields down to the left.

The lane comes up into an open area with roads coming in from the left and the right. Turn left here and follow the road, which will bring you round to run parallel with the N125 (the main road between Lagos and Portimão).

Turn left on the N125 and then take the next turning on the right, next to the village's sports stadium.

9. **(850m)** You're now on the M534. The road surface along the next section is pretty bumpy but it does get better.

Follow the road out into an area of salt marshes until you come to a right turn.

10. **(3.4km)** Turn right at the junction and follow the lane through an area that's mostly fields and open countryside with a few houses dotted around.

Keep going south-east, past a turning for the Palmares golf resort. The road starts to climb – gently at first – as it approaches the back of the villa/apartment complexes overlooking Meia Praia.

The last part of the hill is quite a lot steeper but it's not too long and brings you up to a T-junction in a leafy residential area.

11. **(2.1km)** Turn right on a narrow lane that takes you past a number of private villas set in large subtropical gardens before coming into a much more built-up area.

Keep going straight on, more or less following the ridge, with occasional glimpses of the sea to the left and the Monchique hills in the distance to the right.

The road eventually starts to descend again and you'll see Lagos straight ahead. At the bottom of the hill, go straight ahead (second exit) at the roundabout.

Follow the road straight on, past the Marina Club hotel on the right and around the back of the Marina de Lagos building.

As you come to the end of the marina building, you'll see the old train station to your left. The modern one is a bit further on, beyond the car park.

If you want the centre of town, follow the road to the right and then take the pedestrian bridge over the river. For the centre of Lagos, go left along the riverfront and the historic centre is on the right.

Maps

See **26: Mexilhoeira** (page 199), **12: Lagos centre** (page 80) and **25: Lagos north** (page 198).

MONCHIQUE

Fóia, the highest mountain in the Algarve is only a short ride away from Monchique – but the 902m summit is about 460m above the town.

The mountain top itself isn't that spectacular but the views are wonderful on a clear day. The ascent to the 902m high summit also attracts a lot of local cyclists, who use it as a training ride.

The trip to Fóia described below forms a **17.3km circuit** but you are strongly recommended to take the clockwise route as outlined – going anti-clockwise is a lot tougher.

FOIA ASCENT

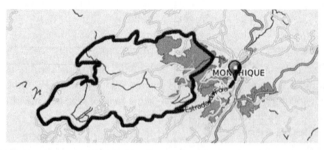

The route starts from the roundabout by the tourist kiosk (*posto de turismo*) at the top of the one-way system around the centre of Monchique.

Stats

Distance: 17.3km
Total elevation gain: +/-506m
Maximum incline: 13.7%

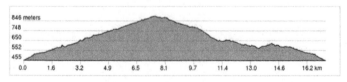

To download a map with full ride profile, available as .gpx file etc., see: ridewithgps.com/routes/7492215

Directions

1. **(5.4km)** Take the exit almost directly opposite the tourist kiosk onto the N266-3, signposted 'Fóia'. You leave town at an altitude of about 440m and the road climbs steadily as it follows the southern side of the mountain.

2. **(2.1km)** There's a viewpoint (*miradouro*) on the left just after you come out of the trees at about 760m above sea level. After this, the road curves around to the north-east for the final climb.

   As you approach the top, turn left towards the radar station, which is the highest point you can reach on the road.

3. **(5.3km)** Return to the junction – the road does a loop around a building housing a craft shop, **snack bar/restaurant** and chapel. Ignore the first right-hand turn and continue north.

   As you head away from the buildings and various masts and aerials, the road begins to drop down several hairpins, losing about 250m in height as it turns east.

   The single carriageway road now follows the northern side of the mountain through forest until you come down to a fork in the road at a T-junction.

4. **(2.7km)** Turn right – back on to a two-lane road – and follow it down and round to the south-east.

5. **(1.8km)** You'll come to a T-junction on the same road that you rode up leaving Monchique. Turn left to descend to the roundabout at the top of town.

Maps

See **2: Monchique** (page 38).

SILVES (STATION)

The landscape to the north-east of Silves is a quiet region of small hills, scattered rural properties and lots of citrus groves.

There's also a pretty good network of country lanes to explore. Some of them are in need of resurfacing but it's also quite easy to escape the traffic of the resort areas to the south.

COUNTRY LANES AND CITRUS GROVES

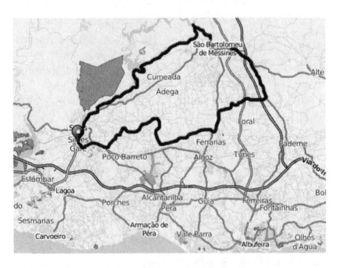

The route described below is a **59.5km circuit** going out to the Arade and Funcho reservoirs and the small town of São Bartolomeu de Messines before looping back to the south and west.

However, it would also be very simple to reduce the distance to just over **47km** if you end the ride at Alcantarilha (the station for Armação de Pêra) and catch the train back to Silves.

Finishing at Algoz station would shave another 4.6km off the total – see below for details.

There are no major hills on this circuit but it's quite undulating in parts so requires a reasonable amount of effort.

The directions below are split into three stages, going to:

- A. São Bartolomeu
- B. Alcantarilha station
- C. Silves station

The complete circuit starts and finishes at Silves station (about 1.5km south of the town itself).

Stats

Distance: 59.5km
Total elevation gain: +/-594m
Maximum incline: 8.5%

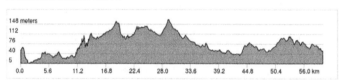

To download a map with full ride profile, available as .gpx file etc., see: ridewithgps.com/routes/7497572

Directions

A. To São Bartolomeu de Messines (25.1km)

1. **(1.5km)** Turn north (left) on the road that crosses the railway at the level crossing.

   Go up the (small) hill ahead, straight on at the roundabout and down the other side – you'll see Silves straight ahead.

   Follow the road to the right as you come down on to the N124-1. There's a wide shoulder at the junction.

   This is replaced by a pavement as you come down the hill but it's a straight road with good visibility and should be safe.

   Keep going down and take the left-turn lane at the junction for Silves – also signposted 'Lisboa'.

   Note: As you come down the hill you'll see a turning to the left leading to an old arched bridge.

You can go this way, which is quite pretty, but the bridge is pedestrian-only and there are steps down on the other side.

2. **(2.5km)** Turn left and go over the Rio Arade towards the junction on the N124, which runs along the other side of the river.

   Bear right as you approach the junction, merge with the N124 and follow the river and its line of palm trees around the south-east side of the town.

Note: There are several **cafés** and a Lidl **supermarket** off to the left as you follow the river around town. For more information on Silves (including accommodation) see page 28.

   Bear right at the next roundabout and follow the N124 north-east away from the town and into the countryside.

   Keep going along a long straight section until you see a left turn, signposted 'Pinheiro Garrado'.

3. **(5km)** Turn left here. The road goes up a short hill,

over an irrigation channel and then curves to the right.

You're now on the M7153, a single-track country road that runs parallel with the N124 for the next 5km.

There are some little ups and downs but this section is all fairly gentle. It's also very rural and quite pretty, although the one thing you might have to watch out for is barking dogs. (My wife and I rode this section in January 2015 and although we didn't get chased by any of them the number of dogs barking at us did get a bit annoying.)

After about 1.9km, the road comes to a bridge over the irrigation channel. Go right to follow the road over the bridge and then bear left – do **not** go straight on.

After 1.1km you'll come to another junction by a bridge. Go left here and follow the road back over the irrigation channel.

The road continues up the valley then turns sharp right and takes you through a shallow ford on the Rio Arade before coming up to a T-junction.

4. **(9.3km)** Turn left on the M124-3. The two-lane road follows the valley north past more fields, orchards and smallholdings, climbing gently towards some rounded hills.

Note: As the valley narrows, the road curves to the right. An unsignposted lane goes off to the left by a large white building. This takes you across the river, past a camper van parking area and up to the *Barragem do Arade* dam.

You can use this as an alternative route. It's about 500m less distance going this way but it's steeper and the road across the top of the dam is cobbled.

After curving to the right, the M124-3 climbs steadily into a small valley surrounded by hills covered with cistus bushes. A tight hairpin bend follows as the road twists around and climbs steadily up to a hill overlooking the reservoir.

At the top of the hill is a junction where the road up the valley meets the road from the dam. Turn right (east) to follow the road – now the M1080 – around the the reservoir.

A small hill follows, after which you drop down into another rural valley, with more fields and orchards between the hills. There are a few short climbs but it's more gentle than around the reservoir.

The last hill on this section brings you up to a T-junction just north of a village with the charming name of Amorosa (which means '*loving*').

5. **(2.3km)** Turn left here on the M1079, signposted 'Passadeiras' and 'Pedreiras'.

The road turns north through some small hills and farmland and comes down to a bridge over the Rio Arade at the top of the Funcho reservoir.

Note: You don't have to continue to the bridge if you don't want to. (Instead turn right at the junction described in **Point 6**.)

However, the area around the bridge might make a good picnic spot as there are several grassy spots down by the water, plus some big eucalyptus trees for shade.

6. **(4.5km)** Turn round on the bridge and go back about

300m to an unsignposted junction.

Turn left up a small, gentle hill and the road will take you south-east through more quiet countryside towards the town of São Bartolomeu de Messines.

As it approaches the town, the road runs parallel with the railway before coming to a T-junction.

Turn left and keep going for 450m along a straight road until you see a no-entry sign ahead.

Go right here, signposted 'junta de freguesia', 'centro do dia' and 'escolas'. Keep going straight ahead and then follow the road as it does a 90° turn to the left on to Rua Manuel Texeira Gomes.

Keep going to another T-junction (Faro and Algoz are signposted to the right). Go left here to head into the town's centre – past an old cinema and a small municipal market building on the left.

You'll see a branch of Banco Espirito Santo (green sign) on the right at a junction signposted 'A2 Lisboa' and 'Alte'.

Note: The church and other older buildings lie straight ahead. However, the town's one-way system is quite complicated and you'll need to come back to this point.

B. To Alcantarilha station (21.3km)

1. **(2.3km)** Turn right towards Alte and take the second exit when you come to a roundabout.

   After 200m turn left at a small crossroads and then right at the next T-junction.

   You're now on a straight road out of town, which will take you under the IC1 and on to a roundabout on the N124.

2. **(1.5km)** Go straight ahead (second exit) on to the N124, signposted 'Salir' and 'Paderne'. The road runs south-east, going under the A2 motorway, and comes to a small roundabout.

3. **(3.8km)** Turn right on to the N270, signposted 'Albufeira', 'Quarteira' and 'Faro'.

   The road starts to descend gently, with a mixture of

olives, figs and oranges among the trees to either side. This is a lovely easy bit of riding, with the landscape opening out ahead of you and very little pedalling needed.

The N270 finally starts to climb again slightly and takes you over a low rise where you pass a large sign marking the border of the Albufeira district.

Keep going down the other side until you see a sign for a turning to Carrasqueira.

4. **(3.8km)** Turn right on to a single-lane road that takes you west through an area with lots of orchards, including more almonds, figs and oranges, as well as pears and carobs.

The road continues roughly west. There are some small ups and downs but no notable hills.

The surface is quite rough in places but you're unlikely to meet much (if any) traffic.

Keep going until you reach a stop sign at a T-junction.

5. **(1.9km)** Go left here. The road wiggles a bit but don't take any side turnings and keep going roughly west until you come to a T-

junction on the N264 just north of a humpbacked bridge over the railway.

6. **(2km)** Turn left on the N264 and over the bridge, going south past large areas of orange groves.

Keep going until you reach a right turn, signposted 'Barranco Longo' and 'Ribeira Alta'.

7. **(3.1km)** Turn right on to on another quiet, almost flat, rural road.

After about 2.9km the road curves to the left. About 150m further on there's a right turn that's almost hidden in the orange trees.

There's no proper signpost but you might see a sign to 'Quinta Uliane'.

8. **(2.9km)** Turn right here and keep going in roughly the same direction. After about 1.8km you'll come to a kind of staggered crossroads (with two roads coming in from the right). Go left and then (in 30m) take the next right.

Keep going straight on and you'll pass a large water treatment complex on the left with white office buildings and lots of flags. Just past here you come to a crossroads on a more major road.

Note: There are few signposts on this section and quite a lot of tiny lanes going off in different directions. But don't panic too much if you get confused.

If you turn right and go north, you should be able to see from the hills inland that you're going the wrong way.

If you turn left and go south, the worst thing that will happen is you come to the N269, which is a more major two-lane road. If this happens, turn right and keep going to the Alcantarilha train station.

9. **(1.1km)** If you want to end the ride at Alcantarilha and catch the train, turn left here.

After about 800m the road goes down a hill and around a couple of bends, bringing you to the N269.

Turn right and the station is on your right in about 100m.

Note: If you are not finishing at Alcantarilha, ignore **Point 9** above and go straight to **Point 1** of the next section.

C. To Silves station (13.1km)

1. **(2.5km)** Turn right at the crossroads mentioned in **Point 8** above and go north, climbing very slightly.

   The road curves to the right and then bends left at the top of a low hill. Keep on north towards a hamlet called Fonte Louzeiros.

   You'll come to a staggered crossroads in the middle of the houses with a small roundabout and a **café** to the right.

2. **(3.9km)** Turn left on the M528. The surface is a bit rough along this single-track lane but it's all quiet and very rural.

   The road runs roughly south-west for about 2.5km then curves south before bending round to the north-east.

   Coming up a gentle hill, you should see a large white building to the left and a junction just in front of it.

3. **(1.6km)** Turn left, signposted 'Montes Grandes'. The road comes up to the top of the hill with excellent views ahead of a rolling landscape covered

with low trees and fruit orchards.

After just under 1.6km there's a turning to the left. Go right and you'll come to a T-junction just around the corner.

4. **(1.5km)** Turn left and go downhill for about 150m to a fork in the road. Go right here. The road goes southeast through more orchards before coming to a junction on the N269.

5. **(1.5km)** Turn right. This is a two-lane road and does get some traffic but is still relatively quiet.

The N269 goes through a low cutting, curving to the right and climbing slightly. Just where the stone banks to either side fade out, there's a turning on the left.

6. **(1.4km)** Go left. Follow the road around a couple of bends and over a two-lane bridge over the railway. Keep going to a T-junction (signposted 'Silves golf' to the left).

7. **(700m)** Turn right on to the M1154. This brings you into a more built-up area with houses to your left.

Keep going and follow the road around a bend to the left. This will bring you a T-junction.

Turn right here and you'll see a level crossing just ahead. Silves station is on the left.

Maps

See **2: Silves** (page 37), **26: Silves station** (page 200) and **15: São Bartolomeu de Messines** (page 122).

ZAMBUJEIRA DO MAR (ALENTEJO)

If you want a day trip up the coast to see some of the most gorgeous coastal scenery in the south-west Alentejo, then this excursion of just over **47km** should fit the bill nicely.

CABO SARDÃO AND ALMOGRAVE

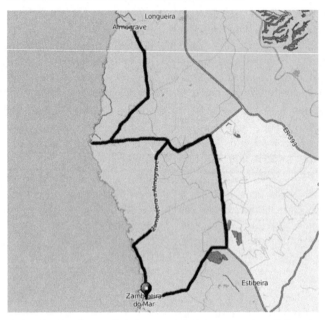

Cabo Sardão has a lighthouse set on spectacular cliffs where (in season) white storks nest on jagged pinnacles above crashing Atlantic waves.

Almograve is a small village with more beautiful beaches and some good swimming spots when tidal conditions are right.

The ride starts from the no-entry sign where the road down into Zambujeira comes to the start of the village's pedestrianised centre.

Stats

Distance: 47km
Total elevation gain: +/-240m
Maximum incline: 2.6%

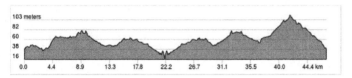

To download a map with full ride profile, available as .gpx file etc., see: ridewithgps.com/routes/7283857

Directions

1. **(2.9km)** Head north from Zambujeira's main street. The road runs roughly parallel to the cliffs, with various boardwalks going out to viewpoints overlooking the sea and the rocks.

   You'll come to a junction where the road ahead descends to a tiny fishing harbour called Porto das Barcas. There are a couple of **café/restaurants** here (generally only open for lunch) and a steep drop to a cove where fishermen land their catch.

2. **(6.4km)** Turn right here, signposted 'Vila Nova de Milfontes'. From Porto das Barcas, the road heads inland across flat farmland, turning north until it comes to a T-junction.

3. **(4.1km)** Turn left, signposted 'Vila Nova' and 'Almograve'. The road runs due west to the little settlement of Cavaleiro but keep going past the hamlet and and you'll soon see the lighthouse at Cabo Sardão ahead (see page 195).

4. **(900m)** From Cabo Sardão, retrace your route and look for a left turn just after you pass a small bar and *mini-mercado* (shop) on your right. Coming back from the lighthouse, there are no obvious signposts but looking towards it there are signs for 'Vila Nova' and 'Almograve'.

5. **(7km)** Turn left here and follow the road north-east

and then turn left again for Almograve.

6. **(800m)** Turn left at the roundabout in the village. There are several **cafés** here (the Estrella do Mar has an excellent selection of cakes), plus a few places to rent rooms if you want to stop overnight.

The road will take you out to a car park just back from a couple of lovely beaches.

There's not a lot of beach visible at high tide but when the sea goes out there are large stretches of sand – and some lovely pools among the rocks to the right for swimming.

Note: The simplest (and shortest) way back to Zambujeira is to retrace your steps.

You could make a bigger loop by going inland and taking the N393 part way but this is a fast, sometimes busy road. It's also quite boring, running dead straight through eucalyptus plantations with nothing to see on either side.

The route below takes a different route after Cabo Sardão, making the return journey about 5km longer than the way out.

7. **(11km)** Go back the same way to the junction near the small bar and *mini-mercado* on the Cabo Sardão road.

Turn left and follow the road east and then south-east to the turning signposted for Zambujeira.

8. **(2.7km)** Continue straight on, signposted 'Odemira'. The road runs south-east and then bends around to the north-east. It will bring you to a T-junction on a bend in a more major road.

9. **(11.6km)** Turn right here and head south on the M502 – there's a **café** on the right after about 1km.

The road continues dead straight and more or less flat (or very gently rolling) through a mixture of woodland, open fields and eucalyptus plantations.

Follow the M502 around a sharp bend to the left and continue on, all the way back to Zambujeira.

Maps

See **4: Zambujeira do Mar** (page 47).

Cabo Sardão and its storks

The white storks at this dramatic headland have adopted several nesting spots in what look like extremely dangerous spots on the cape's rocky crags.

Female storks generally lay a clutch of four eggs during early spring inside large nests built of sticks. These nests can be used for a number of years and often end up well over a metre in height.

Both parents take turns incubating the eggs and feeding the chicks, with the young birds leaving the nest a couple of months after hatching.

Many storks migrate south for the winter, those from Portugal generally heading to tropical sub-Saharan Africa. However, some Portuguese birds stay put, particularly in the Algarve where they can be seen year round.

The stork eats a wide range of animal prey, from insects and fish to small mammals and small birds. It takes most of its food from the ground, among low vegetation, and from shallow water. During daytime they are a common sight in the Portuguese countryside patrolling fields as they look for the next meal.

Even without the storks, Cabo Sardão is well worth a visit for its spectacular cliff and ocean views. There's also a reasonable coast path running along the cliffs here in both directions if you want a bit of a walk.

The 17m-high lighthouse was first proposed in the late 19th century but did not begin operating until 1915. The curious thing about it was that the main building was constructed the wrong way round with the door facing the ocean and the light aimed inland – one suggestion is that the builder had the plans the upside down.

23. Arrifana

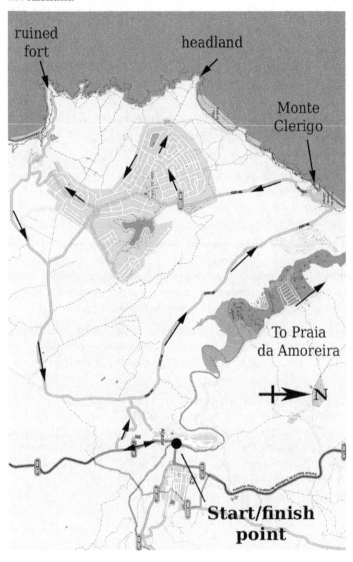

ruined fort

headland

Monte Clerigo

To Praia da Amoreira

N

Start/finish point

24. Boliqueime

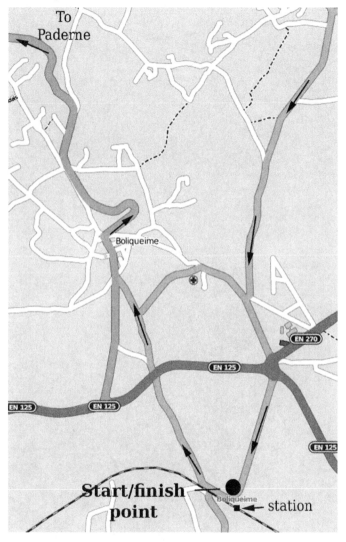

To
Paderne

Boliqueime

EN 270

EN 125

EN 125

EN 125

EN 125

Start/finish
point

Boliqueime

station

25. Lagos north

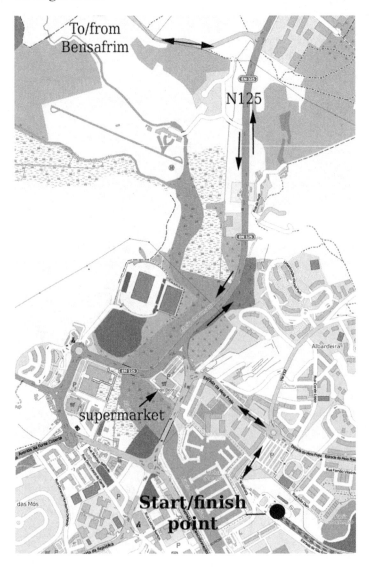

To/from Bensafrim

N125

supermarket

Start/finish point

26. Mexilhoeira Grande

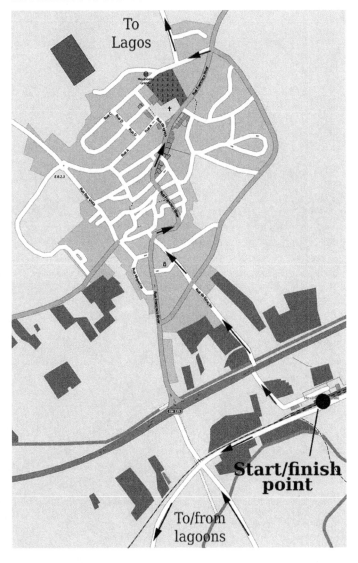

27. Silves station

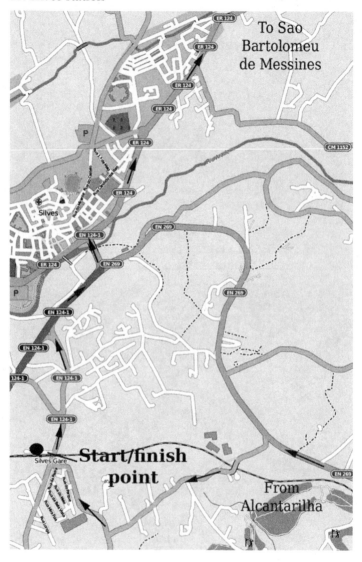

Help keep this guide up-to-date

Thank you for buying – and reading – this guide. Hopefully it's provided you with all the information you need for some superb cycling.

However, this is the first edition of *Cycling The Algarve* and the information in it is based on my own knowledge and research, helped by feedback from other cyclists who have ridden its routes and rides.

To make sure this guide stays fresh and up-to-date, any feedback you can provide would be extremely useful.

If you can add to the information it contains, whether with a recommendation for a guest house, bike shop or somewhere to eat/buy supplies, then please get in touch.

Comments on things to see along the way – particularly if not already mentioned in this guide – are also really useful.

Also, if you find any mistakes or changes (places that have closed, alterations to roads etc.) do please share the information with your fellow riders.

To get in touch:

Email:

pedalportugal@gmail.com

Facebook:

www.facebook.com/pages/Pedal-Portugal

Web:

www.pedalportugal.com – leave a comment on any of the pages.

About the author &
Pedal Portugal

Huw Thomas is a third-generation tandem rider, and novelist, who turned to writing guidebooks on Portugal because he's unable to spend all his time cycling there.

Born in Hampshire, Huw trained as a journalist and worked in PR/communications before finally finding a way of avoiding a 9-5 existence.

A tandem trip around the coasts of France and the Iberian Peninsula in 2004-05 provided his first introduction to Portugal.

After retraining to teach English as a foreign language, Huw and his stoker (wife) Carolyn spent three years teaching in Portugal – an ideal opportunity to explore more of the country and discover a number of excellent bike rides.

During a break in their teaching, Huw and Carolyn embarked on a 10,000-mile tandem ride across 11 countries to raise money for the disaster relief charity ShelterBox.

The experience of planning that journey inspired Huw to set up the Pedal Portugal website to offer advice and ideas to other cyclists coming to the country. Producing guidebooks was the next logical step.

Although now back in England, Huw makes regular return visits to Portugal – using the excuse of needing to keep the website up to date.

pedalportugal.com is now the leading source of information on cycling in Portugal, containing suggestions for a variety of touring routes plus details of day/short rides within Portugal.

Cycling The Algarve is the second in what it is hoped will be a series of Pedal Portugal guidebooks.

Also available

The Alentejo Circuit is based on the popular touring route of the same name, taking in some of the prettiest old towns in Portugal and some of its gentlest cycling.

This six-day route starts and finishes in the historic city of Évora with its World Heritage centre and takes a loop through some of the region's most scenic countryside, visiting the idyllic hilltop village of Monsaraz, a string of castle towns and the southern city of Beja.

It also contains various ideas for side trips and alternative routes, plus the option of a two-day extension taking you out to the best bit of the Alentejo coast (and linking up with the routes in *Cycling The Algarve*).

Acknowledgements

This is the first edition of **Cycling The Algarve** and is mainly based on my own cycling experience and visits to the area.

However, I've also had a huge amount of help from Algarve resident and fellow cyclist Andy Smallwood who knows many of these roads far better than I do.

Andy also leads groups and individuals on guided rides around the central Algarve – for more information see cyclethealgarve.com

I also want to thank Ian Mitchell for generously sharing information on some of his rides – his input helped greatly with the *Alte and Caldeirão Foothills* day ride.

I've also had help from Louise and Frank Russell who test rode part of the touring routes in April/May 2015 and sent back very useful feedback on their rides and stops along the way.

Thanks also to all Pedal Portugal's Facebook friends and everyone else who has shown their support for the book.

Any mistakes in this book are all mine – and if you do discover any then you have my sincere apologies! (Please let me know so I can correct future editions and avoid misleading any future riders).

Also, if you've got any useful information or ideas on cycling in the Algarve that could be used to improve the next edition, please get in touch.

Huw Thomas, June 2015.

Printed in Great Britain
by Amazon

41811915R00116